Dance Choreography for Competitive Gymnastics

Denise A. Gula
Lorain County Community College
Elyria, Ohio

Leisure Press
Champaign, Illinois

Library of Congress Cataloging-in-Publication Data

Gula, Denise, 1949-
    Dance choreography for competitive gymnastics / by Denise A. Gula.
        p.   cm.
    ISBN 0-88011-364-2
    1. Gymnastics. 2. Choreography. 3. Dancing. I. Title.
    GV461.G8   1990
    796.44--dc20   89-12685
                                                                            CIP

ISBN: 0-88011-364-2

Copyright © 1990 by Denise A. Gula

Developmental Editor: Judy Patterson Wright, PhD
Assistant Editor: Timothy Ryan
Copyeditor: Peter Nelson
Proofreader: Greg Teague
Production Director: Ernie Noa
Typesetter: Angela K. Snyder
Text Design: Keith Blomberg
Text Layout: Tara Welsch
Cover Design: Hunter Graphics
Cover Photo: Dave Black
Illustrations: Avis Blum and Denise A. Gula
Interior Photos: Dave Black
Printer: Versa Press

Printed in the United States of America

10 9 8 7 6 5 4 3 2 1

Leisure Press
A Division of Human Kinetics Publishers, Inc.
Box 5076, Champaign, IL 61825-5076
1-800-747-4457

Contents

Preface

It is a generally accepted fact that the dance skills of gymnasts from Eastern Europe far exceed those of gymnasts trained in the United States. Not only do gymnastic programs there seem to take dance more seriously, but the training schedules allow those gymnasts to devote more time to the study of dance.

I strongly believe that the dance needs of the gymnast are very similar to those of the dancer. However, I also believe that the methods for training the gymnast to dance, as well as the manner in which he or she obtains that information, must be altered to fit the specific needs of a gymnastics program.

When dancers work with gymnasts, it is often difficult for them to recognize and acknowledge two very basic situations: the difference in temperaments between dancers and gymnasts and the necessity for a gymnastic program that utilizes an economical system for dance instruction. A dance instructor who is unfamiliar with gymnastics often does not realize how very unique the dance needs of gymnasts actually are; consequently, this instructor may be unwilling to adjust dance training to accommodate these needs. On the other hand, the gymnastic coach who is trained in gymnastics is often unskilled in the highly technical aspects of dance training and, therefore, is unequipped to prepare the gymnast to perform the dance movements required.

For example, a gymnast very often must be able to execute an intermediate- or advanced-level dance skill competently without benefit, usually, of the standard training methods generally used in dance instruction. Unfortunately, there is little opportunity in a typical gymnastic training program for the gymnast to become schooled in the elementary dance techniques that typically lead to these higher level dance skills.

There is yet another problem regarding the dance education of the gymnast. Not only does the gymnast need to be able to execute a variety of upper-level dance skills, but the gymnast must become proficient at several different dance styles as well—a tedious task even for the trained dancer. If, for example, you asked a classically trained dancer to execute a funky jazz combination without previous jazz training, she may

suddenly feel like she has two left feet. One can imagine how difficult it becomes for the gymnast to perform a mixture of dance styles without the appropriate training in those specific disciplines and techniques.

Although I strongly believe that it is necessary for the gymnast to receive dance training, I am completely opposed to teaching the gymnast to dance in the dance studio environment or, for that matter, in a makeshift dance area of the gym. There are a number of reasons for this, the first being that the atmosphere of the dance studio and the gymnasium are as different as night and day. In the gym of a private gymnastic school, there are usually several coaches, each supervising small groups of gymnasts. Various skill-level groups all work at the same time on different pieces of apparatus, with the day's schedule planned on a rotation basis. Each group can spend anywhere from 20 to 45 minutes on an event, depending on the length of the workout and the number of coaches and gymnasts present.

Students are expected to have developed a certain amount of skill in time management and self-discipline. This prevents their standing around and waiting for directions when a coach is occupied with another gymnast. They are also responsible for successfully performing specific skills on, for example, the low beam a certain number of times before practicing those skills on a higher beam. Gymnasts must also have the self-discipline to work a routine repeatedly without just ''blowing it off'' if no one happens to be working with them at the moment.

Because of the gym's fairly relaxed atmosphere, students are free to talk and joke quietly with one another, ask each other for help, and even, with permission, to leave the gym for drinks of water and so on. The gymnast's workout consists of short periods of strong energy output combined with short periods of rest and regrouping. All of this can seem, to the unaccustomed observer, quite similar to a three-ring circus. Despite its apparent confusion and disorganization, though, this setup works—for training a gymnast. It is in fact a remarkably quiet and cooperative atmosphere, considering the amount of activity that is going on at once. All this, in spite of the fact that there may be as many as 25 people in the gym at one time, each of them working, to a large extent, as separate entities.

The dance studio, on the other hand, conducts classes in ballet technique. Instruction is directed to only one group of students at a time, students who have been carefully placed according to age and ability level. There is only one instructor, who is directing at all times the progression of the class, which works in unison as each movement combination is given. Indeed, in a professional school environment (which is the only environment that could be accurately compared to the training environment of the competitive gymnast), the students place themselves completely under the tutelage of the teacher. The entire class works together as a unit: There is no independent study in this environment, everyone begins moving and ends together.

A dance class is 1-1/2 hours long. Dancers spend approximately half of that time at the barre, working exercises that warm up the body, develop technique and turn-out, and condition muscles for the center work that immediately follows. Rest periods are rare: at the barre, perhaps only while the instructor briefly describes the next combination, in center, only when the class is being divided into two or three groups, which then successively perform the given combination. Students are completely discouraged from speaking to each other during class and are not usually permitted to leave the classroom for any reason, unless their intent is not to return. Despite this necessarily highly disciplined atmosphere, a good teacher keeps the class interesting, fast paced, and enjoyable. The most important fact here is that the dance studio system also works—for training dancers.

The only real similarities between these two teaching environments are the dedication of the students and the amount of time they spend in the classroom per week. Even when it comes to these general similarities, the specific differences between the two fields are striking. It is often said that it takes 10 years of daily professional training to produce a dancer. Fortunately, the training of a gymnast can be accomplished in far less time.

Over the years, as I have worked more and more with the competitive gymnast, I have come to realize that simply recognizing the gymnast's unique problems with regard to dance education is not enough. I now believe that what the gymnastics community needs is a practical method for training and developing gymnastics-oriented dance skills. More specifically, what is needed is a method for instructing the gymnast in a dance technique that also encompasses the various aspects of those dance disciplines that are appropriate for gymnastics. It is my hope that the information offered in this text will help make dance more relevant to the gymnast.

Acknowledgments

I would like to express my appreciation to the following people for their help in making this book possible:

my friend Charles P. English III for his ingenuity in creating a method for me to transfer photographic negatives into illustrations;

my husband, Terry, for his photographic help as well as general patience and support throughout this project;

my illustrator, Avis Blum, for her hard work and talent in creating illustrations not available to me from photographs;

Nancy Brensthul, Kathy Koeth, Rae Pica, and my developmental editor, Judy Patterson Wright, for their help and suggestions in the preparation of this project;

and my dear friends Susan Wollerman, for her help in the artwork of this project, and Susan Braig, Jean English, and Barbara Finegan, for their continued loving support and encouragement.

Introduction

This book is primarily concerned with the choreographic elements of floor and beam routines, and is designed to help the reader derive a better understanding of how the choreographic process works. Because many coaches have limited dance backgrounds and because choreography is a natural progression of the formulation of dance movements, it would be a disservice to the reader if this book did not first address some basic information about dance and its relevance to the gymnast.

Therefore, Part I of this book is designed to help the reader gain a broader knowledge of what I refer to as *dance-gymnastics*. Chapter 1 discusses the need for dance-gymnastics and details guidelines for structuring the dance portion of a workout program. Chapter 2, "A Movement Vocabulary for Gymnasts," gives the reader an orientation to dance terms and descriptions, including both the classical and the nonclassical dance vocabularies. This portion of the book may be used by the reader as an easy reference. The various steps and key phrases explained in detail here are used throughout the text in the description of sample patterns and movement phrases. These are all clearly illustrated and defined. Chapter 3 offers some suggestions on class content for incorporating dance elements into the gymnastic workout.

In Part II, "Understanding Choreography," chapter 4 deals exclusively with choreography for the floor, addressing specific elements such as music, structure, floor patterns, required dance elements, and composition. Chapter 5 looks at the various form and content aspects of movement that can make a movement phrase interesting, appealing, and relevant to a routine. Space limitation is obviously a major factor on the beam; therefore, aspects of dynamic balance and control, fluidity, rhythmic variations, and level and directional changes are addressed. Efficient use of space is important in floor exercise, so numerous sample movements phrases are provided, and the effects of movement qualities are addressed. Also included in chapters 6 and 7 are specific guidelines and

choreographic checklists for both floor and beam, respectively. All of Part II will be a helpful guide to follow when first learning how to put routines together.

Part III puts all of the choreographic information together, suggesting phrases that may be helpful in beginning your choreographic work. In chapter 8, various sample movement phrases for competitive floor or beam routines are given. These are described in four distinctively different styles: classical (ballet), folk, jazz, and contemporary. A movement phrase will be given in one style (classical, for example); then, whenever possible, the same phrase will be repeated, but stylistically altered so that it fits one of the other movement styles (such as jazz). In instances where it is not possible to alter a phrase to fit another style, it will be labeled only for the most appropriate one.

Chapters 9 and 10 will help you begin to choreograph your own movement phrases. In chapter 9 you are given a particular group of skills and asked to compose a movement phrase using the music, movement style, tempo, and floor pattern given. Following each of these problems, a sample solution is suggested to help you. In chapter 10 the problem-solving approach is again used for composing your own balance beam phrases. In this chapter a movement experience is described. You are then asked to develop a phrase based on movements that could describe that experience. Again, sample solutions are suggested for easy reference.

The information and material developed in this text are intended not only to familiarize you with dance but also to teach the basic principles and techniques behind the development of a student. With this information you can better determine how dance may become a workable addition to the training program of gymnasts. It is my hope that through the use of this material, you will discover previously unthought-of movement possibilities, while making dance more meaningful and relevant to your gymnasts.

Introduction

PART I

The Need for Dance Training Awareness

In order to be better prepared for competition, the gymnast must be trained early on in dance technique. For this reason it is vital that members of the gymnastic community educate themselves as to the mechanics of dance. However, coaches must not lose sight of the fact that traditional methods of dance training were developed many years ago for the sole purpose of producing highly skilled and artistically expressive dancers—not gymnasts. It is thus up to the gymnastic community to research dance technique and find ways of making dance more relevant and applicable to the gymnast. This means learning which elements of the art form are absolutely essential to the gymnast's development and performance, and adjusting the application of these elements to better serve the gymnast's needs.

Is Dance Technique Relevant to the Gymnast?

Much of dance technique is highly stressful and can be damaging to very young bodies. This danger is primarily associated with the strain on joints and tendons that results from forcing a 180-degree turn-out. A secondary problem, boredom and disinterest, may result from the tedious repetition of many isolated movements at the barre. All this training is of course vital to the development of dancers. However, because of the potential problems, the dance community by and large does not recommend serious classical ballet training for children under the age of eight.

Keeping this in mind, it is important for the gymnastic community to understand that elements such as 180-degree turn-out and repetitious barre movements certainly carry the same risks for the young gymnast that they do for the very young dancer. And,

while these elements may be an integral part of the dancer's development, they are in their pure, "classical" form quite unnecessary for the development of the gymnast.

Which Dance Principles Are Relevant?

In order to execute dance steps correctly, the gymnast requires some basic understanding of the principles of dance technique, namely, proper body placement, the ability to work "through" the feet, the use of an aesthetically turned-out leg, and correct use of the *plié*. Beyond this, the gymnast needs to increase his or her dance vocabulary to make a wider range of movements available and to thoroughly understand the mechanics of the most commonly used dance steps. This will help ensure proper execution of the dance elements in a routine and will also contribute to the continuity and flow of all dance movements. The end result will be an improved overall artistic presentation and expression in the gymnast's performance.

Identifying Teaching Goals

If dance instruction for the gymnast is to succeed, it must be taken out of the dance studio and adapted to the gymnasium. Coaches and dancers who work in the gymnastics field must recognize that the ultimate goals of dance education for gymnastics students are not the same as those for dance students. Further, they must realize that although a command of the principles of dance technique is essential if the gymnast is to perform floor and beam routines with artistry and style, these principles cannot be taught in the same manner that they are taught to the dancer.

What, then, should the goals of a coach be when incorporating dance into the gymnast's training program?

1. Basic Instruction in Dance Technique

The gymnast must have a strong basic understanding of dance technique in order to perform movements with proper amplitude, *that is, ease and fluidity*. The competitive gymnast will benefit tremendously from a training program that emphasizes proper execution of all dance movement skills because early detection

of bad habits will save a great deal of grief that would otherwise come later.

2. Work Dance Skills and Movement Combination Often

The gymnast is required to include some specific dance skills and connecting steps in floor and beam routines. Introducing a movement/dance vocabulary early in your training program will provide your gymnast with the necessary tools for composing optional floor and beam routines.

3. Always Stress Performance Quality in Executing Dance

In their presentation of dance, competing gymnasts must transcend a level of merely correct execution (the movement being performed with technical accuracy) to reach a level of artistic expression (the movement being performed with style, finesse, and aplomb). The more often the gymnast performs dance, the more comfortable he or she will be with the movement styles. Having developed sufficient kinesthetic memory for the execution of dance movement skills, the gymnast will be able to concentrate on the performance quality.

Gymnastic training programs that incorporate dance movement skill work on a regular basis produce gymnasts that are comfortable with the performance of dance elements in competitive programs. For these goals to be achieved, the gymnastic community in general must recognize its need for dance.

To a very large extent, that recognition has already begun. In *Coaching Women's Gymnastics* (1984), Bill Sands states:

> The most important tactical decision a coach can make about the dance in floor exercise is that gymnastics has not even scratched the surface of what dance has to offer floor exercise. Our approach to the dance of floor exercise is largely two-dimensional: score and consistency. Only a few gymnasts have stepped into the realm of actually dancing in floor exercise rather than simply executing the movements that are taught. Again, the climate of gymnastics is to produce gymnasts fast and assembly-line the champions. The extensive and intensive learning necessary to perform the dance portions of the floor exercise take many years. We should all increase our knowledge about the dance areas that are so important to floor exercise. Increased appreciation of the

subtle nuances of the dance should improve floor exercise as an event. In this country there are few people knowledgeable about the dance of floor exercise. We should encourage them and emphasize this portion of our floor exercise routines to enhance all facets of the event. (p. 174)*

In his discussion of dance skills and the balance beam, Sands has even stronger criticism:

In my opinion, the path international gymnastics is taking on balance beam is not in keeping with a very artistic approach. The balance beam should be theatre on a stick. It should be floor exercise elevated above the floor. It should be a question of elegance, art, creativity and movement. What we are developing on balance beam is a wooden tightwire act that has no redeeming characteristics other than risk. After all, if the gymnast were to perform a single tuck back on the floor in her floor exercise routine, everyone would be sick. The only redeeming characteristics of a tuck back on balance beam is its risk. I may have allowed a tactical blunder by allowing gymnasts to perform skills that are more dance-oriented and easily more difficult and fall-producing than a tuck back, but I do not believe that balance beam should continue on the path it is going. Elegance has been sacrificed in the name of difficulty, crucified on the cross of "risk." (p. 171)*

*From Coaching Women's Gymnastics by B. Sands, 1984, Champaign, IL: Human Kinetics. Copyright 1984 by Bill Sands. Reprinted by permission.

CHAPTER 1

Dance-Gymnastics

Now we get to the crux of the problem: How do we teach the gymnast to perform dance successfully without the benefit of a classroom atmosphere expressly designed for teaching dance? And, having recognized the need for dance training, how do we fit it into the workout schedules of gymnasts?

I believe the answer is first to adapt dance to meet the needs of the gymnastic environment. Then the gymnastic community must focus on raising a generation of gymnasts whose training reflects, from the very beginning of their gymnastics experience, the successful integration of elementary dance skills and technique. In addition to this, colleges and universities must recognize the need for teaching courses in dance technique and kinesiology as well as in dance-gymnastics. These must be designed not only for the college competitor but also for the future coach.

Teaching the Gymnast to Dance

It is time to think of dance as an integral part of the gymnast's training. Frequently, when an outside dance person is brought into the gym, his or her work with the gymnasts is seen as something separate from the other action taking place during the workout. Dance is often thought of as merely an additional element, helping put the icing on the gymnast's cake. Instead, from the beginning of training, it should be an integral part of the total program, just as work on vault or bars are integral to the total training process.

Dance Training: An Essential Ingredient

It is commonly accepted that strength and power are both necessary components for work on bars or vault; therefore, gymnastics training programs are designed to include exercises that develop these skills. Portions of the program that accomplish this are not thought of as mere add-ons, extraneous to the core training of the gymnast. Rather, they are considered essential ingredients in the development of strong, competitive gymnasts. Why, then, should a format that develops the artistic and technical aspects of dance execution be considered extraneous?

Dance Training for the Gymnast: How Is It Different?

Once we recognize that dance training must become an integral part of the overall gymnastics training program and that the presentation of this material must be altered for the gymnast, it is time to examine exactly what the dance needs of the gymnast are. To do this, it is again necessary to look at the differences between dance and gymnastics to see how dissimilar their teaching goals are.

The goal of the dance teacher in the professional school environment is to train students exclusively in the art of dance, imparting to them unlimited knowledge of steps and technique. Let's take it a step further and consider the end result of these efforts—the performance. It is fairly safe to say that in a piece of concert stage choreography, the average length of a solo dance might be about 4 to 8 minutes. Also, all of the movements within that particular piece of choreography would be dance related.

The goal of the coach on a gymnastic team, on the other hand, is to train gymnasts in tumbling, vaulting, beam, and floor skills. The result of that work is the gymnastic competition. In competition the gymnast is expected to perform a piece of choreography the length of which is a maximum of 1-1/2 minutes. In such a piece, only a portion will draw on dance-related material for its content.

Although the basic subject matter for the dancer and the gymnast remains the same, their individual needs with regard to that matter are very different. Therefore, when we ponder the idea of teaching dance and the gymnast's acquisition of dance knowledge, we must recognize which areas of traditional dance training are relevant. If we can clearly determine this, we can more easily adapt dance training for the gymnast.

Fitting Dance Into the Workout Schedule

Gymnasts want and need dance training. The question is, How can the gymnast best receive that training? It is ludicrous to assume that one can take the traditional dance format out of the dance studio and force it to function successfully in a gym environment. It is equally ludicrous to think that the gymnast can benefit from or be happy in a traditional dance class even once a week.

What then is the answer? Before we can begin to integrate dance training into a gymnastic program we have to recognize that what the gymnast wants to do is tumble! If it were dance that the gymnast was interested in, he or she would already be in the dance studio, not the gym. Next, we have to identify exactly what the gymnast's dance needs are, recognizing that the gymnast is already physically out of sync with the intellectual understanding of dance. This is perhaps the most difficult aspect of integrating dance training into a gymnastic program. The normal process of teaching dance assumes that the student is physically at a beginning level and simultaneously develops both the body and the intellectual understanding of dance at the same rate; this is possibly the first indication that perhaps the methods of dance instruction for the gymnast need to be altered. Finally, we have to package this information as concisely as possible and present it to the gymnast in a relevant form that is applicable to the workout schedule.

Incorporating Dance Into the Gymnastic Program

There are a number of possible ways in which dance can be included in the workout schedule. Generally speaking, though, there are two basic methods that can be followed: the rotation method and the separate dance session.

Rotation Method

Rotating among beam, vault, bars, floor, and dance is probably not a very desirable method, because the time designated for dance is so limited. However, it is a start and can be beneficial if the material presented remains focused and relevant to the gymnast's needs.

Separate Dance Session

This is the more desirable method because the entire class time can be devoted exclusively to working on the necessary dance elements. The session should meet once a week. Dance elements and sequences that are appropriate for both floor and beam routines should be included in the practice time.

Incorporating Dance Into the Competitive Team's Program

Within these two different approaches there are a number of ways in which dance can be incorporated into the workout program. Precisely which way will depend on whether you are planning a gymnastic lesson (class) or a team workout schedule.

Rotation Method

This approach will be effective only if your team works out at least 2-1/2 hours several times a week. In such a schedule, divide your gymnasts into groups according to skill level. Rotate them to different events every 25 minutes.

Another type of the rotation approach is to split the team into two groups. One group spends the first 1-1/4 hours rotating between beam, vault, and bars; the other group remains on floor, working both dance and tumbling skills. Halfway through practice the groups switch positions.

Separate Dance Class

Gymnasts are assigned to one dance class a week in addition to their normal workout schedule. Class time should be at least 45 minutes to an hour, with a class 1-1/2 hours long being ideal. The benefit of this arrangement is in the larger block of time allotted to dance.

If you find it impossible to fit a separate dance session into your workout schedule, consider combining the two methods for a more effective program. Incorporate dance into your rotation schedule on a regular basis, but once a month include a separate dance session to work exclusively on dance skills and technique.

Incorporating Dance Into Gymnastic Classes

Again, the dance lesson plan will be somewhat different depending on whether you are planning for a dance rotation or a separate class.

Rotation

Obviously, in a setting where gymnasts receive instruction for as little as 1 to 1-1/2 hours a week, there is little time to work all areas of the gym. In this instance, particularly at a beginning level, much of the dance work will have to be incorporated into both the warm-up and the conditioning portions of the class as well as into the floor and beam rotations.

While working floor, gymnasts can practice individual dance skills and movement combinations. These are easily incorporated into basic tumbling work. Simple drills that combine two or more dance skills, such as *chassés* and split leaps, can be practiced. Movement phrases that incorporate dance elements with basic tumbling skills are also effective, for example, *chassés*, *tour jetés*, and back roll extension. These are very helpful in teaching the gymnast to move smoothly from tumbling to dance and vice versa.

During the beam rotation, repetition of dance skills that are performed on a straight-line path should be stressed. In lower learning levels, this is perhaps even more productive than working beginning-level tumbling skills that require close, one-on-one attention from the instructor.

Your gymnasts can be given a list of dance movement skills, such as *chassés*, *pirouettes*, *assemblés*, which they are asked to practice in succession as individual skills and also in combinations as movement phrases. These should be worked first on the floor, then on the low beam, and finally on the high beam. Emphasis should always be placed on correct execution as well as fluidity and continuity of movement.

Performing movement skills in this manner will enable the gymnast to first develop some confidence in movement expression on the balance beam before being asked to incorporate the more difficult tumbling skills. Very often we see competitive gymnasts who have conquered difficult and impressive tumbling skills in their routines but appear awkward and unsure of themselves as they attempt the simplest dance movement. Incorporating more movement skills into the beam portion of the workout can help to correct this problem.

At the end of the workout, certain aspects of dance can be included into the gymnast's regular conditioning. Many coaches, for example, ask their gymnasts to perform a certain number of push-ups or abdominal exercises as part of their conditioning program. Conditioning exercises that improve and develop certain dance skills such as scale or *arabesque* may also be incorporated on a regular basis.

Separate Dance Session

Another possible approach is to offer in your program three levels of dance-gymnastics classes. In this approach, students who are registered in your regular gymnastics program are encouraged to also register for dance-gymnastics class. These gymnasts are then assigned to the appropriate levels and encouraged to attend this class once a week along with their regular instruction.

This is an ideal approach for a number of reasons. First, the beginning gymnast, who is not yet involved in a demanding and consuming competitive workout schedule, has far more time to devote to a dance-gymnastics class. With tumbling skills still fairly limited, this is a level at which the gymnast can begin to develop some very sound dance technique. Second, the gymnast is able to learn correct technique from the beginning of gymnastic training instead of developing bad habits that will later have to be broken should he or she continue seriously with gymnastics. Finally, the gymnast who grows up with dance will feel more comfortable with it. Such a gymnast is less likely to resent the addition of dance later on; in fact, it will require less time, allowing the gymnast to continue to develop and concentrate on gymnastic skills.

All of this means that when ready to begin competition, the gymnast has dance skills more on a par with his or her gymnastic skills. Remember, however, that the emphasis here is on dance-gymnastics, not traditional dance work. Your students should be able to focus strictly on dance skills that are required of the gymnast. At beginning levels, it is also an opportune time to begin working on some of the dance phrases required in compulsory routines, both on floor and beam.

One final thought: Obviously, there is more to learning how to dance than just perfecting the individual skills and steps. Therefore, it is important that regardless of how dance is incorporated into the program, the gymnast must have sufficient time during each session to work not only individual dance skills but also movement phrases that combine both dance and gymnastic elements. Naturally, the gymnast should be coached regularly on dance technique, such as placement, upper torso carriage, and presentation, during each practice on beam and floor, not just during times designated for dance. Each session should contain creative combinations that employ all styles of dance tempos, rhythms, and types of movements. These need to be combined in a manner that is appropriate for floor and beam routines. There are many examples of these in chapter 6. Most gymnasts really enjoy working dance elements when they are combined with floor work, falls, and acrobatic skills. When the dance skills are integrated with acrobatic and gymnastic skills as they are in competitive floor routines, the gymnast has an opportunity to see how relevant all of this really is to the performance. Changing the combinations each meeting gives the gymnast an opportunity to be exposed to a wide variety of movements that ultimately help develop his or her own creative potential.

Summary

Because dance is an art form with a large vocabulary and varied styles, it is never too early to begin training young gymnasts in the fundamental skills and techniques of dance. Addressing this area of study early on will allow the gymnast to acquire and incorporate dance and gymnastic skills simultaneously. Furthermore, if a dance-gymnastics program is to be successful and effective, the dance and gymnastic communities must both recognize the differences between teaching dance to dancers and teaching dance to gymnasts. Even within the filed of dance, there are notable differences in both the approach and the material between training classical ballet dancers and training modern dancers or even jazz/theatre dancers. Someone attempting to learn classical ballet skills within the structure of a jazz class, for example, would meet with little success. Because training a gymnast to dance is not the same as training a dancer to dance, it is necessary that dance be customized to fit the unique needs of the gymnast.

CHAPTER 2

A Movement Vocabulary for Gymnasts

There are many excellent technical dance manuals and classical ballet dictionaries available on the market. Unfortunately, these are generally written for dancers who are assumed to have a working knowledge of the subject already. This means that in some instances the gymnastically oriented reader may find the information somewhat sketchy. In other cases, the gymnast may find the text more thorough or technical than seems relevant. There are some subtleties, however, regarding dance technique with which the gymnast should become acquainted. These are general rules that, once understood, may be applied to the execution and performance of all dance movements.

Elements of Dance Technique the Gymnast Should Learn

The following are important elements of dance technique and can improve gymnasts' overall execution.

Turn-Out

Turn-out refers to the rotation of the leg outward from the hip. This positioning of the leg in the hip socket generally creates a more pleasing line for most dance movements. For the gymnast a functional amount of turn-out is probably only 90 degrees, as opposed to the dancer's ideal, 180 degrees. A gymnast's 90-degree turn-out should be sufficient to give a well-turned-out leg that, in an extended or pointed position, is aesthetically pleasing to the eye. Ninety degrees is also enough for properly executing any of the dance steps that may be required. In fact, for much of the gymnast's work, particularly that performed on the beam, a turn-out beyond 90 degrees may actually be detrimental.

Placement

Correct *placement*, body alignment, is required for proper execution of dance steps. It is also an integral part of understanding the mechanics of those steps as well.

Specifically, placement is the positioning of the ribs, abdominal muscles, the hips, and the spine while executing all movements of dance. Positioning is important for dance movements on the floor, but critical on the balance beam, where proper alignment ensures a steady performance of movements.

Holding and keeping the body in proper alignment while performing dance movements is extraordinarily difficult for a student untrained in ballet technique. Indeed, one purpose of a traditional ballet barre is to help the beginning student not only develop turn-out, as previously mentioned, but also find and hold correct body placement. In a dance class this is accomplished through the execution of a daily 45-minute barre workout, which allows the student to focus exclusively on correct alignment throughout each progressive exercise. Obviously, in a gymnast's workout schedule, time is at a premium. Therefore, we need to find a way for the gymnast to understand correct placement without having to go through the rigors of a traditional 45-minute ballet barre.

One way to help the gymnast find and maintain correct alignment is through the use of imagery. My personal favorite image is the "spring coil." I first ask the gymnast to stand with feet in a parallel position (heels and toes together). Then I ask the gymnast to feel the abdominal muscles pull up and inward to make the pelvis "straight," neither pressed too far forward (overemphasizing the natural curve of the spine) or pressed too far backward (eliminating the curve of the spine altogether). I also ask that the muscles on the inside of the thighs be contracted so that a general tightness is felt in the whole pelvic area, and that the chest be lifted upward and the shoulders relaxed.

The gymnast should then imagine that I have about 20 spring coils like the kind in upholstered furniture; these are fairly stable coils, unlike those of, say, the Slinky® variety. Next, I ask the gymnast to imagine that we are going to place some of these coils between the bottom of the ribs and the top of the hip bone. Once the first one is in place, we are going to inset the remaining 19 coils at equal distances around the entire waist like a belt. (Keep in mind that these coils are inserted *between* the ribs and the pelvis, not around the outside of the waist.) What we hope to happen is that the gymnast lifts the chest up, extending an *equal* distance between ribs and pelvis all the way around.

Because these are spring coils, the gymnast still has complete freedom of movement in all directions. The movement is therefore both controlled and extended. Invariably, there will be some gymnasts who, in an effort both to imagine the coils between the hips and ribs and to lift the chest, also hike up the shoulders. Emphasize that the shoulders must stay relaxed and that although the chest is lifted, all tension is transferred to the waist.

After giving the exercise, test the gymnast's placement by standing in front and putting your right hand on the gymnast's left hip and your left hand on the right shoulder. While applying resistance to the hip, attempt to push the gymnast sideways by pushing against the shoulder. If remaining stable, the gymnast has achieved the correct alignment, properly engaging the oblique and rectus muscles. These muscles are absolutely vital in holding the position once the gymnast is placed. If the gymnast has not engaged these muscles, ask him or her to place his or her own hands on the space between the hips and the ribs and to feel what happens to the muscles during a cough. Now the gymnast places the index fingers at the sides of the waist and pushes in while coughing again. If the oblique and rectus muscles are engaged, the gymnast will feel their resistance. Explain that this is the feeling that should be in the midsection when the gymnast imagines placing spring coils between the pelvis and the ribs.

Once the gymnast understands the muscular action necessary for maintaining this alignment, find some key phrase to remind him or her of correct placement, such as "Check your center." You will find using this kind of key phrase while coaching very valuable, especially when the gymnast is working on the beam, where proper alignment is essential to consistency and balance in the dance elements.

Beware of the Injunctions "Tuck Under" and "Pull Up"

Certain catch phrases have been used in the teaching of dance that, unfortunately, have been misunderstood and have contributed to the misalignment of two very important areas.

Pelvis tucking generally means placing the pelvis in a position correctly aligned with the upper torso and the rest of the body. Unfortunately, the student usually responds to the instruction "Tuck under" by pressing the pelvis forward by contracting the gluteal muscles, at the same time strongly pulling the abdominal muscles in. All of this, rather than achieving correct alignment, actually causes the pelvis to tilt backward. This positioning of the pelvis destroys the natural curve in the spine, which must be maintained at all times.

When the pelvis is tucked under like this, the quadriceps are overworked, which can contribute to bulkiness in them. When positions such as high extensions to the side are held, tucking can place an undue amount of strain on the Y ligaments, contributing to a condition known as "rider's strain" (Y ligaments are those fibers surrounding the hip joint that resemble an inverted letter "Y"). Knee ligaments can also be overstretched, lessening their ability to protect the knees from possible injury.

When the pelvis is tilted forward, an extreme curve in the low back can be seen. It is not uncommon to see gymnasts, particularly very young ones, assume a stance that emphasizes such a curve in the spine. Perhaps this is because they so frequently use an arched back position to perform tumbling skills. Unfortunately, they very often become so accustomed to the extreme curve that it prevails through all other movements they perform. If this position is not corrected, it may result in stress, strain, and pain to the low back area, particularly if it is held during dance movements. In more severe instances, it may contribute to curvature of the spine.

The gymnast generally responds to the injunction "*Pull-up*" by sticking out the ribs while also tilting the pelvis forward. This causes stress in the upper lumbar and lower thoracic areas of the spine. It also displaces the center of gravity, causing strain in other areas of the body. Ideally, instead, the pull-up implies an extension of the spine through the neck, creating space between the hips and the ribs so that the chest is lifted while the ribs remain closed. This position is then held by engaging all abdominals, both the oblique and the rectus groups.

Working Through the Foot

Learning to work through the foot while executing dance movements not only enhances the aesthetic quality of the performance but also improves the execution of most dance skills. In all dance steps where a brushing action initiates the movement, a full stretch of the foot is needed. As the foot is seen to disengage from the floor, strong muscular action is required so that the toes may extend outward as the heel lifts from the floor first, followed by the metatarsals, and finally the toes. In a return action, the exact reverse takes place: The tips of the toes touch the floor first, then the ball of the foot, and finally the heel.

The gymnast is aware of the necessity for a well-pointed foot but needs to perform exercises that help develop the muscular coordination and strength of the instep and the metatarsals. Here are two very simple exercises that the gymnast can do while sitting at home talking on the telephone or watching television. They are done in bare feet and with the aid of a pencil or a marble.

1. Place a pencil on the floor. Instruct the gymnast to lengthen and extend the toes out from the metatarsals so that they are lying flat over the pencil. Then curl the toes around the pencil, attempting to pick up the pencil from the floor.
2. Place a marble on the floor. Instruct the gymnast to attempt to ''wrap'' or ''cup'' the metatarsals and the toes around the marble and pick it up.
3. Instruct the gymnast to sit on the floor with the legs extended in front of the body in a pike position and the feet strongly flexed so that the back of the knees are on the floor and the heels are lifted off the floor. Next, while keeping the toes flexed, the gymnast should extend the metatarsals forward so that the heels of the feet are contracted toward the calves and the feet are stretched. Finally, the gymnast should extend the toes out and downward toward the floor until the feet are fully pointed. This exercise should be repeated several times.

Understanding Basic Dance Elements

All dance steps are simply a combination of very basic movement elements. Application of the movement principles will greatly enhance the overall dance movement performance. This section identifies some of the most important elements and provides definitions, teaching hints, and developmental drills to help gymnasts' performances.

Plié (plee-AY)

Pliés help keep the joints and muscles pliable and the tendons flexible and elastic. In all *pliés*, the legs must be well turned out from the hips, the knees must remain open so they are directly over the toes, and the weight of the body must be equally distributed over both feet so that the entire foot is flat and grasping the floor.

In a traditional ballet class, *pliés* are usually the first exercises given. The students are asked to perform them first in *demi-plié*, a half bending of the knees, then in *grand plié*, a full bending of the knees. The exercise given is generally of fair length (approximately 5 minutes) and is repeated in all five positions of the feet.

The purpose of the *plié* exercises in a ballet class is to (a) serve as a total-body warm-up; (b) strengthen the legs; (c) reinforce turn-out in the hip socket; and (d) develop kinesthetic memory (muscle memory learned through repetition of a specific movement or skill) through the correct use of all muscular actions required to maintain that turn-out throughout various dance steps. Although the gymnast must understand this action and learn to use the *plié* correctly, he or she does not have the time to practice this exercise in the traditional dance manner.

The proper execution of *pliés* are also necessary for better landings from the gymnast's jumps, smoother connections in dance steps, and improved powers of rebound. Because of the need to ''stick'' landings in gymnastic routines, the gymnast is accustomed to stopping the bending action of the knee in *plié* position. This is fine when landing from particular gymnastic skills. Unfortunately, the gymnast usually transfers this particular kinesthetic memory to *all* dance movements that end in a *plié* position as well. This interrupts the natural flow of the particular movement, which inhibits its correct execution, giving the movement a choppy or disjointed appearance.

Skill Developmental Drills: Plié

To learn to keep the action of a *plié* smooth and continuous, the gymnast should practice jumps performed in a series. This forces the gymnast to use the legs in a springing fashion—the most important element of a *plié* during landing—and also requires continuous motion during the ascent and the descent of the *plié*—the most important aspect of creating smooth connections between steps. A jumping series might consist of the following progression: straight jump, tuck jump, double stag with right, double stag with left.

Teaching Hints: Plié

- Instruct the gymnast to be sure that the heels come completely to the floor between jumps. The tendency to jump from a slightly raised heel can contribute to tendinitis in the ankle area.
- The gymnast must fully straighten the knees to push off the floor. This helps propel the body upward.
- Do not let the gymnast "grip" the thighs on the landing. This could completely stop the motion and could contribute to overdevelopment of the thighs, could strain the knees, and could interrupt the necessary continuous flow of movement. Rather, the gymnast should reach the lowest point of the *plié* and immediately begin the ascent; this happens whether performing the next jump or the last. At no time should one stop at the depth of the *plié* before straightening the legs.

Tendu (tahn-DEW) and Dégagé (day-gah-ZHAY)

These movements are the leg's disengaging from a closed position to an open and stretched position. In *pointe tendu* the weight remains on the supporting leg while the working leg stretches outward to the front, side, or back with the toes remaining on the floor. A *dégagé* is basically the same action, but the toes lift slightly off the ground.

The purposes of *tendues* and *dégagés* as barre exercise are to

1. develop and strengthen the instep;
2. define the musculature of the lower leg;
3. improve the coordination and control of many ballet steps that begin with the disengaging of the leg from fifth position; and
4. build speed for quick footwork, such as required by multiple jumps.

Although several of these purposes are applicable to the gymnast, it is not necessary for him or her to perform these exercises in the traditional classroom manner. Instead, stretching the feet and developing the arch, along with coordinating a well-turned leg, can be accomplished by a series of walking steps performed in a circle.

Skill Developmental Drill: Tendu and Dégagé

Ask your gymnasts to form a large circle. Then, moving to music in either a clockwise or a counterclockwise fashion, they should perform the following:

a. Walking steps with swinging arms, feet pointed and toes touching the floor first. (The accent is "down" on the first beat.)
b. Brushing steps with arm swings and fully stretched feet. (The accent is "out" with the brush on the first beat.)

Teaching Hints: Tendu and Dégagé

- When stepping forward onto the leg, the gymnast should brush the bottom of the foot along the floor until it is fully stretched and pointed. The gymnast should feel as though there were something sticky on the bottom of the foot that he or she is trying to brush off.
- As the foot disengages from the floor, the toes should be fully pointed, the heel contracted at the ankle and engaging the muscles of the calf.
- As the weight is transferred forward, the gymnast should step through the foot (onto toe, ball, then heel of the landing leg). The emphasis is on correct alignment of the torso and using the arms as in a pendulum swing.

Skill Developmental Drills: Triplet

A variety of musical tempos is also helpful. While your gymnasts are still in a circle formation, these walks might be followed with triplets. A triplet is a series of three steps performed to a waltz tempo. The first step is the largest and is performed on the downbeat, or Count 1 of the music. The next two steps are generally smaller and performed successively on Count 2 and Count 3. (Take a large step forward onto the right leg. Your knee should bend and your foot should be slightly turned out as you take the step. Next, step forward onto the ball of the left foot with a straight leg, then forward again onto the ball of the right foot with a straight leg.)

Teaching Hints: Triplet

- On the first step of the waltz, emphasize the use of the *plié* as a smooth transitory element connecting the first step to the second step.
- On Counts 2 and 3, the gymnast should show the fully stretched leg in a high *relevé* (rel-a-VAY) position, raised onto the ball of the foot. A pleasing turn-out of the leg should be seen as well, along with pleasant upper body carriage, lifted focus, and a strong brush of the foot.

Rond de Jambe (rohn duh zhahnb)

This is a circular movement of the leg that may be performed either with the toes of the foot touching the floor or with the leg extended so that the foot is off the ground. When performed as an exercise at the barre, the foot describes a full half-circle by extending and pointing directly in front of the body, opening to the side, continuing to the back, and finally closing under the body again. Both legs must be kept straight, and all movement must come from the hip.

The purpose of the exercise is to loosen the hips while maintaining turn-out and correct body alignment. When performed off the ground with the working leg at at least a 90-degree angle to the torso, the exercise is helpful in developing strength in the legs.

In a traditional ballet class this exercise is done slowly and at the barre. In center work it is done as an *adagio* exercise, one of several performed in succession that consist of slow, graceful movements and are used to develop strength, poise, and balance.

Skill Developmental Drill: Rond de Jambe

One way for the gymnast to practice this exercise is to slowly take the leg to the front and hold it at a height of about 45 degrees, then smoothly carry the leg to the side position while raising it to a height of approximately 90 degrees. (In this position the hips must remain straight to the front, and the knee of the working leg must face toward the ceiling.) From the side position and attempting to maintain the leg at the same height, at least, as established to the side, the gymnast slowly begins rotating the leg in the hip socket while carrying the leg to the back in *arabesque* position (one leg is held at a right angle to the body). The gymnast must be sure to allow the chest and upper torso to adjust slightly forward as the leg rotates to the back. This is necessary to give the leg enough room to make the transition from side to front without jamming in the hip socket.

Teaching Hints: Rond de Jambe

- The supporting leg must remain straight, and the hips must not tuck under in an attempt to get the leg to a height above 45 degrees.
- Be sure that the torso remains properly placed throughout the exercise and that the abdominals are well pulled up. Ask that the gymnast feel fully extended both up and down from the center of the torso: through the spine to the top of the head, and to the floor while emphasizing a stretched support leg and a fully anchored base heel.
- Here is a helpful image to use when rotating the leg from side to back: The gymnast imagines standing next to a platform that is about 3 feet high. When the leg is extended to the side position, the leg should feel extended above this platform. Now, as the leg rotates in the socket to make the transition from side to back, it must not dip down but must remain elevated so that it does not at any time touch the platform.

Développé (day-vlo-PAY)

The *développé* is a slow, sustained unfolding of one leg in any direction to maximum height. In a turned-out position, one leg is lifted, sliding up the supporting leg until the toe of the raised leg is touching the knee of the other leg. Then, the gymnast still maintaining the turn-out, the raised leg opens through *attitude* position (knee bent at 90-degree angle with knee higher than the foot) to the front, the side, or the back. From this open position, the leg continues to move outward until it reaches its fullest extension.

The purpose of this exercise is to develop control, balance, and flexibility. This is an invaluable exercise for the gymnast, although it, like the other exercises, does not need to be practiced in the traditional way.

Skill Developmental Drills: Développé

1. The gymnasts execute walking *développés* as they continue to move in their circle formation. This may be performed with the arms extended to the sides, stepping first on a bent support knee, then a straight leg, and finally on a straight leg in a high *relevé* (rel-a-VAY), raised onto the ball of the foot.
2. Another way to practice this movement is as a conditioning exercise at the end of the workout session. One gymnast stands holding onto the balance beam or a wall while a partner lifts the first gymnast's leg to a high, bent position in front or to the side of the body. The leg is then extended to a straight position and held. The gymnast doing the exercise must be sure to maintain correct posture. Once the height of the leg has been established, the gymnast can attempt to lift the leg away from the support of the partner. The position should be held for a slow count of 5.

Teaching Hints: Développé

- The most common technical error when performing a *développé* is to allow the supporting knee to buckle and the pelvis to tuck under while trying to extend the leg to its maximum height.
- Another technical error frequently seen is allowing the knee of the working leg to drop as it

extends. Rather, whatever height is established by the knee as the leg rises to the front must be maintained as the leg straightens. The torso remains fully lifted throughout the movement.

Body Positions in Classical and Nonclassical Dance

There are three ballet methods commonly used in instruction today. They are the French School, the Russian School, and the Cecchetti School (the Italian School). Although there are some minor differences among these methods, specifically in the naming of certain positions and poses, the only significant discrepancies that concern the gymnast are in the naming of arm positions. Adhering to any one particular method when referring to these arm positions is not practical for the gymnast. Therefore, what are shown in the following illustrations are positions that give the gymnast the widest range of possibilities and that in fact reflect a mixture of the three different schools of ballet.

Classical Arm Positions

The classical ballet arm positions are shown in Figures 2.1 to 2.8. In classical ballet the arms are never straight. Rather, the elbows are slightly bent so that there is a natural curve to the arms. In Figure 2.2, for example, where the arms are held in second position, you can see that the arms are slightly rounded, the elbows lifted, and the palms facing outward. In general, when executing any classical ballet arm positions, the torso should be held with proper ballet placement: abdominals "well pulled up," ribs "lifted and closed," shoulder blades "down toward the waist," spine "lengthened," sternum "lifted," and pelvis "straight."

This text will use classical ballet position terms to indicate arm placement for most movements. If, for example, the movement called for in the choreography

Figure 2.2.   Second position.

Figure 2.3.   Fourth position—French School.

Figure 2.4.   Fourth position low.

Figure 2.1.   First position.

Figure 2.5.   Fourth position middle.

Figure 2.6. Fourth position high.

Figure 2.7. Third position or high fifth.

Figure 2.8. Fifth position low.

indicated second position placement of the arms, they would be extended in this rounded position.

Nonclassical Arm Positions

When a nonclassical arm position is called for in one of the choreographic phrases, this text will refer to traditional gymnastic arm placements to identify that position, for example:

- *Sideward arm positions*—anytime the arms are extended directly to the side of the torso and parallel to the ground.

- *Forward and backward arm positions*—when the arms are extended directly forward or backward from the torso and parallel to the ground.

Keep in mind that the arm position given always refers to the placement of the arm in relation to the position of the torso. For example, in Figure 2.9 the left arm is forward middle and the right arm is high.

When nonclassical arm positions are called for, they may also be described in the following manner:

Figure 2.9. Left arm forward middle; right arm high.

- *Straight*–No bend in the elbow.
- *Curved upward*–A slight bend of elbow with palms facing up (see Figure 2.10).
- *Curved downward*–A slight bend of elbows with palms facing down (see Figure 2.11).
- *At right angles*–A 45-degree bend of the elbow (see Figure 2.12).
- *Box position*–Arms placed together at 45-degree angle in front of chest or over head to form rect-angle (see Figure 2.13).
- *Full contraction of arm*–Elbow bent so wrist and hand are pressed to shoulder (see Figure 2.14).
- *Parallel high fifth*–Both arms extended overhead in straight, parallel position (see Figure 2.15).
- *Parallel forward with upward curve*–Both arms forward middle and parallel, but curved so that elbows face down with palms upward toward ceiling (see Figure 2.16).

Port de Bra (por duh BRAH)

Port de bra refers to the carriage of the arms, meaning the movement or series of movements made as the arms pass from one position to another.

Arm Movements in Classical Positions

The manner in which arms are moved from one po-sition to another, *port de bra* adds flavor to the overall

Figure 2.10. Arms curved upward.

Figure 2.11. Arms curved downward.

Figure 2.12. Arms at right angles.

Figure 2.13. Box position.

Figure 2.14. Arms at full contraction.

Figure 2.15. Parallel high fifth.

Figure 2.16. Parallel forward; upward curve.

look of the movement. In classical ballet this carriage is always smooth and graceful. The arms should be softly rounded, with the torso and the head inclined in a complementary fashion. As the arms lift to begin a *port de bra*, they generally pass through what is often called "the gateway," or first position. The *port de bra* is then generally finished by lowering the arms in line with the sides of the torso.

There are a number of possible *port de bra* movements. The Cecchetti method presents a set of eight specific exercises, two of which are illustrated here (see Figures 2.17a-i and 2.18a-g). These are offered to show how effectively the classical *port de bra* movements can be used not only to train the gymnast in graceful arm carriage but also to increase the gym- nast's awareness of the movement potential for this part of the body. Keep in mind that the *port de bra* movements may be used successfully not only when accompanying a specific step but also independently during a pose on floor. As long as the torso is signif- icantly engaged, *port de bra* movements may also be performed on the beam as an independent movement.

Figure 2.17.   One example of Classical *Port de Bra* movements.

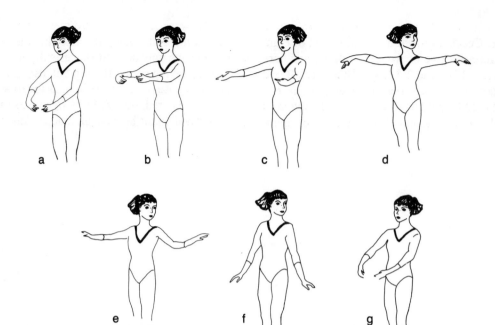

Figure 2.18. Another example of Classical *Port de Bra* movements.

Arm Movements in Nonclassical Positions

The manner in which arms are moved in modern or jazz dance *port de bra* is not nearly so limited as in classical ballet because the traditional placement of the soft, slightly curved arm does not have to be maintained. Examples of nonclassical *port de bra* movements are shown in Figures 2.19 to 2.28.

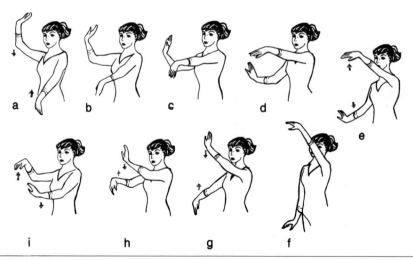

Figure 2.19a-i. Snake arms forward.

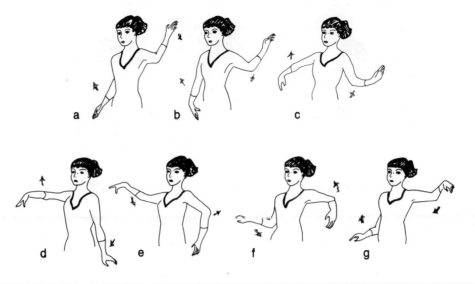

Figure 2.20a-g.   Snake arms to the side.

Figure 2.21a-h.   Figure eight side to side.

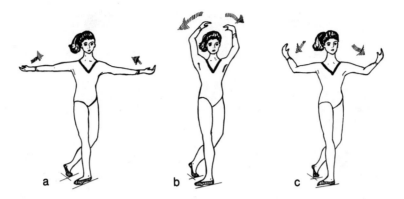

Figure 2.22a-c.   Figure eight over head.

Figure 2.23a-f.   Sunburst.

Figure 2.24a-c.   Lasso.

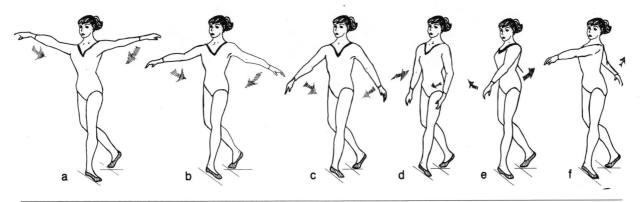

Figure 2.25a-f. Pendulum swing, front and back.

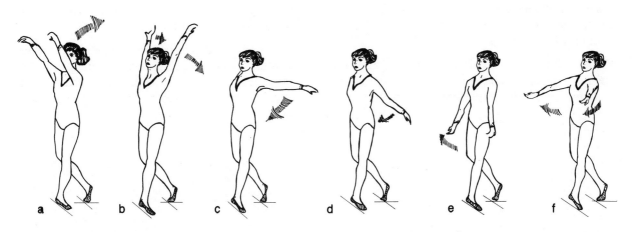

Figure 2.26a-f. Full circles, front and back.

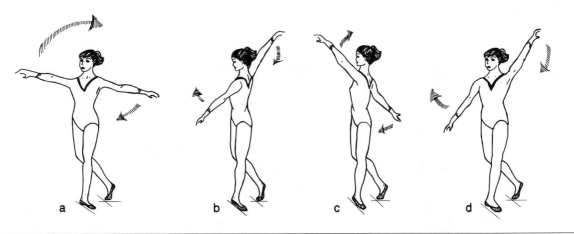

Figure 2.27a-d. Windmill, front and reverse.

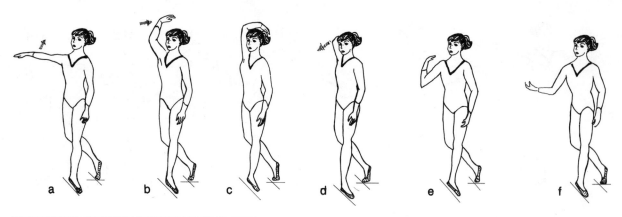

Figure 2.28a-f. Overhead arm sweep, side to side.

Some words describing how arms may be moved through these various *port de bra* movements include the following:

Press. This means to offer resistance against the air, for example, with the palm of the hand as the arm changes positions (see Figures 2.29a-i).

Movement example: Arms held in high fifth position, *press* to second position.

Movement description: From a high fifth position, the arms straighten and turn so that the palms face outward. From this position the elbow bends so that the palms move downward in line with the shoulders.

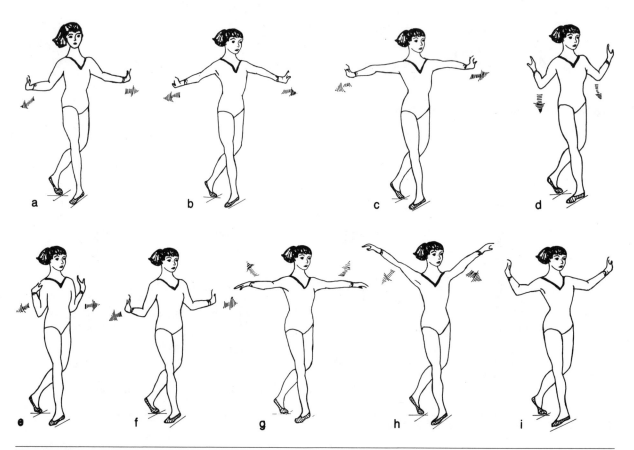

Figure 2.29a-i. Press.

This is immediately followed by straightening the elbows so that the arms press forcefully into a straight-arm second position; the hands are flexed at the wrists and the palms press out against the air. There is a feeling of lift through the torso, particularly in the chest, as the arms move from fifth position to second position.

Cut.   This refers to a particular use of the hand in relationship to the torso. The hand is turned so that the palm faces up and is held in a firm position; the fingers are straight and touching. The hand is cut into the body by bringing the palm inward while moving the elbow out. As this is done, the torso responds with a contraction (see Figures 2.30a-d).

Movement example: Step to second position jazz lunge *cut* right arm to ribs

Movement description: Standing in parallel first position with arms in straight second position, step with the right leg to a parallel side lunge (right knee

bent). Simultaneously, the right hand cuts toward the ribs, sharply twisting so that the palm is facing up and quickly moving toward the rib cage, while the elbows bend and the torso contracts. Notice that the hand does not actually touch the body.

Slice.   This movement also emphasizes the position of the hand, but its action is *away* from the body instead of toward the torso and a contraction (see Figures 2.31a-c).

Movement example: With arms in fourth position front, *slice* right arm to straight second position.

Movement description: Standing in a forward lunge position with your right leg forward, place your arms in middle fourth position. Slice your right arm to a straight second position: From a curved front hand position, flip your hand so that the palm is facing down and the fingers stiffen and extend. The side of your hand then forcefully slices through the air, straightening the elbow as your arm moves to second position.

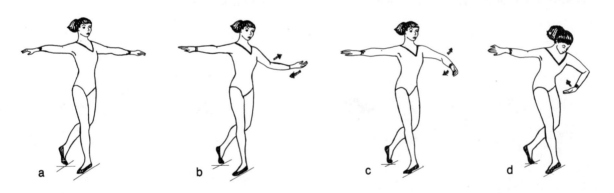

Figure 2.30a-d.   Cut.

Figure 2.31a-c.   Slice.

Scoop.   For this movement the hand is cupped, and the movement engages the entire arm and shoulder area. The action is similar to scooping ice cream out of a round container (see Figures 2.32a-g).

Movement example: From fourth position lunge with arms in middle fourth position, _scoop_ right arm to second position with upward curve.

Movement description: Stand in fourth position lunge with right leg front and arms placed so they are both extended out to the side in second position. Lift your right hand up at a 45-degree angle so that the fingers face outward and the hand is cupped. Now press the hand back, down, and in toward the side of the body with the elbow out (lower the hand slightly as you bring it toward the side of your body), then invert the arm so that it scoops to an upward curved second position.

Classical Positions of the Feet

There are five foot positions in classical ballet and every step or movement begins or ends in one of these positions. In Figure 2.33 the feet are shown with the heels together and touching and the toes turned outward. Figure 2.34 shows the feet placed in the same position as Figure 2.33, but with the heels at a distance of one and a half the length of the foot, shoulder-width apart.

Third position and fifth position of the feet (as seen in Figure 2.35) are often used interchangeably. Although the most common reference is to "fifth" position, "third" position is illustrated here because it is the more "relaxed" placement of the two, it is generally more appropriate for the gymnast. According to both the French and the Russian schools, for fifth position to be performed correctly requires that the heel of the front foot touch the toe of the back foot and the toe of the back foot touches the heel of the front. In the Cecchetti method, the feet are also crossed and touching each other, but the first joint of the big toe shows beyond either heel. Gymnasts usually find the more relaxed crossing of third position to be more desirable for most movements. Figure 2.36 shows the feet in fourth position. In this position one foot is placed in front of the other while both feet remain turned out.

Figure 2.32a-g.   Scoop.

Nonclassical Positions of the Feet

The nonclassical positions are not applicable to ballet movements but are used to perform most jazz and some contemporary movements. The positions would also be used when performing movements on the balance beam. Figure 2.37 shows the heels and toes of the feet placed together. In Figure 2.38 the feet are approximately hip width apart and in Figure 2.39 one foot is placed in front of the other but the feet are still parallel.

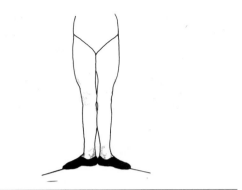

Figure 2.33. First position.

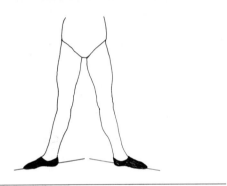

Figure 2.34. Second position.

Figure 2.35. Third or fifth position.

Figure 2.36. Fourth position.

Figure 2.37. Parallel first position.

Figure 2.38. Parallel second position.

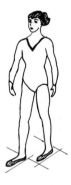

Figure 2.39. Parallel fourth position.

Positions of the Torso

Body positions are useful in describing many jazz and contemporary dance movements. In Figure 2.40 the torso is in a contracted position; the abdominal muscles are strongly pulled inward so that the hips are tucked and the ribs are closed together. In Figure 2.41 the upper body is arched backward. A side arc position (Figures 2.42a, b) indicates that the torso is curved to the right or left. Figure 2.43 shows the torso in a forward tilt position, meaning that the torso is held in a straight line, or position, but the body inclines forward at an angle from the hips.

Some Static Positions

Figures 2.44 through 2.62 demonstrate some classical and nonclassical positions commonly used in dance.

Figure 2.42a-b.   Side arc right and left.

Figure 2.40.   Torso contraction.

Figure 2.43.   Forward tilt (lunge).

Figure 2.41.   Upper torso arc.

Figure 2.44.   Side dig.

Figure 2.45. Back dig (open).

Figure 2.49. *Passé* turned out.

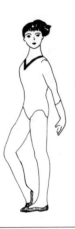

Figure 2.46. Parallel *coupé*.

Figure 2.50. *Passé* parallel.

Figure 2.47. *Coupé* front.

Figure 2.51. Forward lunge with forced arch.

Figure 2.48. *Coupé* back.

Figure 2.52. Forward lunge with pronation.

Figure 2.53.   Parallel side lunge with twist.

Figure 2.54.   Hip lift.

Figure 2.55.   Forward layout.

Figure 2.56.   Side layout.

Figure 2.57.   Back layout.

Figure 2.58.   *Attitude* front.

Figure 2.59.   *Attitude* side.

Figure 2.60. *Attitude* back.

Figure 2.61. *Arabesque allongée.*

Figure 2.62. *Arabesque penchée.*

Turns

The gymnast is required to use turns in both the floor and beam presentations. Descriptions of some typical turns that might be used follow.

- *Outside pirouette* (peer-oo-WET)–This is a turn performed away from the supporting leg, also called an *outside turn*. If one is asked to perform

an outside turn on the left leg, the right leg would be placed in *retiré* position (leg turned out with toe placed at knee), and the turn would be to the right, *away* from the turning left leg.

- *Inside pirouette*–This is the exact reverse of the outside turn. In the case of a turn called for on the left leg, the right leg would be lifted to *retiré* position, and the rotation would be to the left, *in* toward the turning leg.
- *Attitude* (ah-tee-TEWD)–*Attitude* refers to a body position where one leg is raised to the front, the side, or the back; held with a bent knee at an angle of 90 degrees; and well turned outward, the knee higher than the foot. To execute a turn in this position, take a pivot on the support leg in either an inside or an outside rotation.
- *Arabesque* (ah-ra-BESK)–This is a position of the body where one leg is raised to the back and held at a right angle to the body. A turn in this position could be taken on a bent or a straight support leg.
- *Coupé* (koo-PAY)–This turn is performed as a *pirouette* with the free leg pointed and placed in a turned-out position at the ankle, either in front or in back of the support leg. It may also be performed in a parallel position, which is very common for the gymnast. In this case, it is placed at the ankle but beside the support leg so that it is parallel.
- *Renversé* (ron-ver-SAY)–This means to turn outward in a raised position. Step forward onto the left leg into a lunge position. Immediately step under and behind the left leg, with the right quickly lifting the left leg forward into the air. Immediately carry the leg to the side and back before stepping down onto it behind the right foot. Then unwind to the lift by pivoting around one rotation, ending with the left leg in front.
- *Spiral*–This refers to the placement and action of the upper torso during a turn. Begin standing on the left leg, placing the right leg behind, with the arms crossed in front of the body and to the left. Move the arms through the middle front position to the side. As this is done, the part of your torso above the waist pulls off the body's center so that it inclines in the direction of the arms. Continue moving the arms to the right, allowing them to travel back and diagonally upward, arching the upper back into the position. As this is done, begin to pivot to the right one full rotation. As the rotation is completed, the arms also complete their full circle by moving diagonally upward and back to the left, finishing to the side middle position, where they began.

- *Hip circle*–This turn is performed in the same fashion as the one previously described. However, instead of the shoulders and upper torso moving in a circular fashion outward from the body's center, the hips move this way while the shoulders remain centered. It is also possible to combine these two turns so that the upper body begins the spiraling action and is soon followed by the hips.
- *Soutenu* (sue-tin-NEW)–Extend the right leg to the side and spring onto the leg in a *relevé* position raised onto the ball of the foot. Immediately cross the left leg tightly in front of the right so that the legs are seen in a X position. Then unwind to the right with one rotation of the body.

Moving in Space

Following are dance steps that are appropriate for gymnastic work. To help you with their application, each is identified as being appropriate for use on either floor, beam, or both. A brief definition tells how each movement is performed, and, where applicable, variations of that movement are included. Although most of the steps are of the ballet genre, keep in mind that by adjusting the arm and torso positions, you may fit any of these steps to other dance styles.

Arabesque allongée (ah-ra-BESK ah-lwan-ZHAY)
[Appropriate for floor]

This is a scale taken so that the head, hips, and extended leg are on one plane. The arms are generally held in parallel straight-high fifth position, and the base leg may be either bent or straight (refer back to Figure 2.61). It requires a great deal of movement control to get in and out of this *arabesque*.

Arabesque Promenade (ah-ra-BESK prawm-NAHD)
[Appropriate for floor]

This is a slow turn on one leg in the position of *arabesque*. It is accomplished by pivoting on the ball of the support foot while successively lifting the support heel just slightly off the ground and pressing it inward toward the raised leg. This action is performed smoothly while the established height of the leg and lift of the torso are steadfastly maintained.

Arabesque Penchée (ah-ra-BESK pahn-SHAY)
[Appropriate for floor or beam]

First establish the body in *arabesque* position. Then immediately flex at the hip of the support leg to lower the torso toward the standing leg. Once there, begin the recovery to the starting position. Be sure that the relationship of the leg to the hip does not change as the torso is lowered. As the torso returns to the beginning position, the raised leg may lift higher than its original height.

Assemblé (ah-sahn-BLAY)
[Appropriate for floor or beam]

Step onto the left leg in *plié* position. Immediately brush the right leg forward about 45 degrees and simultaneously straighten the left knee as you push up into the air. While still in the air, allow the legs to come together in a tightly crossed position. Land on two feet in third position with the knees bent (see Figures 2.63a-e).

Variation: You may also perform an *assemblé* while turning.

Figure 2.63.   *Assemblé.*

Balancé (bah-lahn-SAY)
[Appropriate for floor or beam]

Balancé, considered a typical folk dance step, is also known as a *waltz step* or a *triplet*. Step to the side with the right leg and bend the knee. Cross the left leg behind the right and step onto the ball of the left foot while straightening the left leg behind the right and raising slightly off the right. Transfer the weight back onto the right leg, bending the knee. This step is performed to a 3-count:

- Count 1 corresponds to the side step to the right,
- count 2 corresponds to the cross back step with the left, and
- count 3 corresponds to the last step taken on the right.

Figures 2.64a-k show the *balancé* to both the right and the left sides.

Variations:

1. Large, sweeping step to the side with twisting of arms and torso. This should be performed in a smooth, lyrical fashion.
2. Short, quick jump onto foot as you begin. This is performed in a brisk, lively, coquettish fashion.
3. Turning. This is actually two waltz steps performed consecutively. The first waltz step travels forward as a triplet (down, up, up), and the second waltz step pivots as it is taken to rotate either one-half or one full turn. This particular movement could be performed on a straight path and used on the balance beam.

Figure 2.64. *Balancé.*

Ballonné (bah-loh-NAY)
[Appropriate for floor or beam]

The translation of *ballonné*, which can be used as a folk dance step, is "bounced like a ball." Step forward onto the left leg into *plié*. Brush the right leg forward approximately 45 degrees and straighten the left knee to jump into the air. (This much is similar to the be-ginning portion of an *assemblé*.) As you begin to land onto the left leg in *plié*, simultaneously bend the right knee so that the foot comes to the ankle of the left leg (*coupé* position). Immediately upon landing, remain in *plié* with the left leg and extend the right leg back out to 45 degrees. The brushing leg appears to beat at the ankle before extending back out to 45 degrees (see Figures 65a-e).

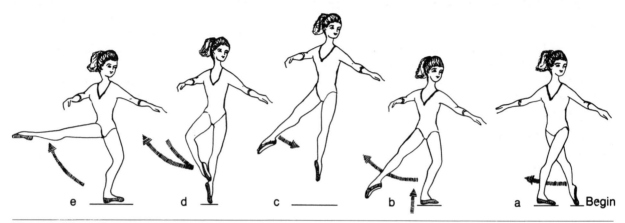

Figure 2.65. *Ballonné.*

Ballotté (bah-loh-TAY)
[Appropriate for floor or beam]

Ballotté may be translated as "tossed." Begin standing on the right leg, with the left pointed to the back. Bend the right leg and straighten the knee as you spring into the air, drawing the legs together under you. Land with the left leg in the spot vacated by the right and perform a small *developpé* with the right leg to the front as you land, the torso leaning slightly backward away from the tossed leg (see Figures 2.66a-d). Now spring up into the air again, taking off from the left leg and drawing the right leg to the left underneath you. Again, land in *plié* on the right leg in the spot vacated by the left foot and execute a quick, small *developpé* with the left foot to the back. This time the torso leans forward away from the tossed leg.

Figure 2.66. *Ballotté.*

Balançoire (ba-lahn-SWAHR)

[Appropriate for floor or beam]

This step is like a seesaw, performed forcefully with a continuous swinging motion. Stand on the left leg and point the right foot to the back. Place the arms in high fourth position (right arm in high fifth and left arm in second). Forcefully brush the right leg to the front above 90 degrees and lift the chest as you tilt the torso back slightly, and turn the head to the right. Now allow the right leg to lower; immediately brush it back as high as possible as you allow the torso to tilt slightly forward while changing the arms so that the right arm extends to straight middle and changing the focus to look out over the fingers of the right hand. Allow the movement to bring at least one more leg swing (that of the leg coming forward again) before you move on to another position (see Figures 2.67a-d).

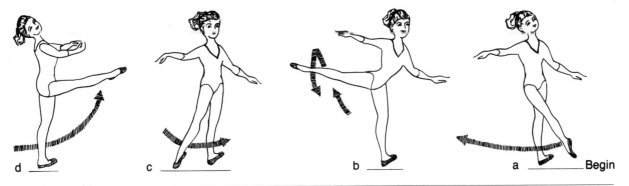

Figure 2.67. *Balançoire.*

Brisé (bree-ZAY)

[Appropriate for floor or beam]

Step and *plié* on the left leg. Immediately brush the right leg to the side about 45 degrees and simultaneously straighten the left knee as you push up into the air. While still in the air, forcefully bring the legs together, the closing left leg appearing to chase the other. Then immediately beat the back (left) leg to the front, the legs quickly exchanging places, or beating, just prior to the landing, which will be taken on both feet. This is essentially an *assemblé* that is beaten (see Figures 2.68a-d).

Figure 2.68. *Brisé.*

Cabriole (kah-bree-OHL)

[Appropriate for floor or beam]

Take a preparatory step forward on the left leg. Swing the right leg forward into the air and immediately spring upward off the left leg by pushing strongly into the ground and straightening the left knee. This leg then beats under the right leg, sending it higher into the air as the landing takes place on the left (see Figures 2.69a-e).

Variation:

1. *Cabriole* may be performed with the beat either to the front or to the back.
2. *Cabriole fouetté* (kah-bree-OHL fewh-TAY) is a step performed basically as described above, but with the body turning a half-rotation away from the beat to land in an *arabesque*.

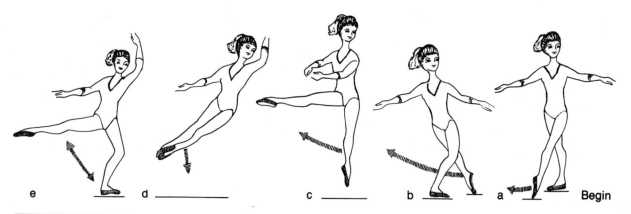

Figure 2.69. *Cabriole.*

Coupé-jeté Turning (koo-PAY zhuh-TAY)

[Appropriate for floor]

Spring up into the air, taking a half-turn to the right. Land on the left leg with the right foot in *coupé* front position. Continue turning to complete a rotation as the right leg swings forcefully into the air for a long and low split leap. This leap is performed very quickly and should appear to "dart" (see Figures 2.70a-g).

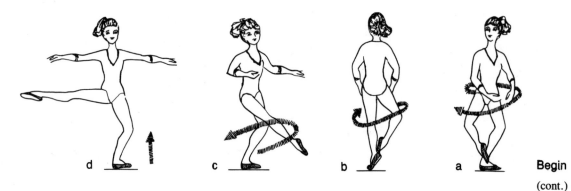

Figure 2.70. *Coupé-jeté* turning.

(cont.)

Figure 2.70. (Continued)

Detourné (day-toor-NAY)
[Appropriate for floor or beam]

Stand on the right leg, with the left leg extended to the back in a low *arabesque*. *Plié* on the right leg and turn halfway to the left, rotating the left leg in its socket so that it is now front. Straighten the right knee as you complete the half-turn. Figure 2.71 shows the movement beginning with the left leg pointed to the front and swinging backward into the *arabesque* position before executing the *detourné*.

Variation: Make one full turn. *Plié* on the left leg, then straighten to *relevé* as you turn halfway to the right (your left leg remains in *arabesque*). Now rotate the right leg in its socket so that it is also the front leg. Continue turning halfway to the right, maintaining this leg position.

Figure 2.71. *Detourné.*

Emboité Turning (ahm-bwah-TAY)
[Appropriate for floor]

Begin standing with the feet in fifth position. Jump into the air, turning halfway to the right. Land on the left leg in *plié*, with the right foot placed in *coupé* position at the ankle. Forcefully jump up into the air again so that the legs are once again straight and crossed as you rotate halfway to the right. The landing this time is on the right leg in *plié*, with the left held in *coupé* position at the back of the ankle (two jumps equal one rotation). This sequence is shown in Figures 2.72a-g.

Figure 2.72. *Embôité* turning.

Fouetté (fweh-TAY)
[Appropriate for floor and beam]

Fouetté means "whipped"; this step is a sharp whipping around of the body from one direction to the other. Take a preparatory step onto the right leg. Immediately kick the left leg forward to the front. At the height of the kick, pull the left leg away from the hip so that it rotates in its socket as the torso whips away to the right. The left leg ends in *arabesque* (see Figures 2.73a-d).

Variation: A *fouetté* may be performed on a straight leg in *relevé* or as a hop.

Figure 2.73. *Fouetté.*

Pas de Basque (pah duh BAHSK)

[Appropriate for floor]

For this typical folk dance step, begin standing in third position *relevé*. Bend the right knee and extend the left leg to the front and across the right leg, then the leg circles to the left side. Transfer the weight onto the left leg, stepping into *plié* and straightening the right leg. Now move the right leg from the side to the front, stepping onto it in fourth position. Close the left leg to third position back. This is a 3-count movement performed with the timing of a waltz (see Figures 2.74a-g). Step to the side on count 1. Take the left leg forward and step onto it in fourth position on count 2. Close the right leg into the left into third position on count 3.

Variation: A *pas de basque* may be performed more briskly with a hop. In this case, the hop is taken onto the first step in second position.

Figure 2.74. *Pas de basque.*

Pas de Bourrée (pah duh boo-RAY)
[Appropriate for floor]

This step, as with most that are appropriate for folk dancing, originated as a country dance step. It is three steps taken traveling in any direction. Starting in third position, extend the right leg just off of the ground to the side, the left leg going to *plié*. Return the right leg to third position front, rising onto *relevé* with both legs. The left leg steps to the side, and the right leg closes in third position back (see Figures 2.75a-d).

Variations:

1. Step back, side, back.
2. Step back, side, front.
3. Step front, side, back.
4. Step front, side, front.
5. For turning, step back with the right leg, make a half-turn to the right as you step onto the left leg. Pivot a half-turn on the left leg to the right side as you close the right foot front.
6. For running, step forward onto the right leg in *plié*. Run forward onto the left leg, then forward onto the right. This triplet has a down, up, up appearance.

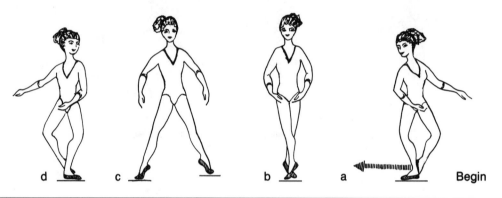

Figure 2.75. *Pas de bourrée.*

Sissonne (see-SON)
[Appropriate for floor and beam]

Begin in third position. *Plié* and spring upward, opening the front leg forward to land on one leg. The second leg may either close to third position or remain open in a low *arabesque* (see Figures 2.76a-c).

Variation: A *sissonne* may be taken traveling forward, sideways, or backward.

Figure 2.76. *Sissone.*

Tour Jeté (toor zhuh-TAY)

[Appropriate for floor or beam]

This is very simply a forward hitch-kick with a rotation so that the second leg swings immediately backward into *arabesque*. Begin in *arabesque* on the left leg and take a preparatory step backward onto the right leg. Rotate the body 1/2-turn to the right. Kick the left leg forward. Jump up and scissors-kick the right leg as you rotate a half-turn to the right. The landing is on the left leg as you immediately swing the right leg backward and up to *arabesque* (see Figures 2.77a-e).

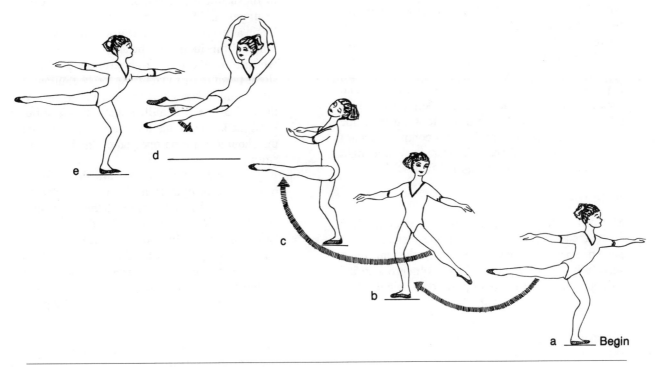

Figure 2.77. *Tour jeté.*

Pas de Papillon (pah duh pah-pee-YOHN)

[Appropriate for floor or beam]

This is literally the "butterfly step." Step forward with the left foot into a fourth position lunge with the weight on the front leg. Scissors-kick the legs to the back, the arms undulating from side to side like butterfly wings while the body curves back. Land on the right foot, in *arabesque* and immediately slide the left leg forward to the fourth position lunge on the landing (see Figures 2.78a-f).

Figure 2.78. *Pas de papillon.*

Jazz Slides

[Primarily appropriate for floor; in some instances, may be adjusted for work on beam]

Forward Slide

This slide is much larger than a side-to-side jazz slide and should begin with a preparatory step to lend force to the movement. Take the preparatory step forward with the right leg, then step forward with the left. Forcefully kick the right leg front and above 90 degrees while keeping the arms down by the sides and lifting to diagonal back position (the palms face down). As this is done, the upward thrust of the right leg propels the body just slightly off the ground and forward, so that the placement of the left foot has shifted from the sole to the top of the foot. At the same time, the chest is lifted as the arms continue upward to end in a diagonally back V position with a slight upper back arch. Your focus is lifted.

Side-to-Side Jazz Slides

Step on the left foot across the right. Simultaneously swing the arms from parallel left side position, down and up to parallel right side position. At the same time, forcefully lift the right leg 45 to 90 degrees to the side and twist the torso slightly to the right while scooting to the right on the base leg.

Some Falls

[Appropriate for floor]

Falls can be executed in several directions and from many positions. Following are descriptions of some falls that may be used by gymnasts.

Backward Fall

Starting position: Stand with the left leg in plié and extend the right leg pointed to front, the arms in diagonal back V position with upper back arch.

Movement sequence:
 a. Extend the torso to straight position, bringing the arms to high parallel fifth position. Continue sweeping the arms forward in parallel circles so that the torso contracts and the head focuses in toward the stomach. The left leg remains in plié, with the right leg extended forward.
 b. Shift the body weight far forward so that the weight gently transfers onto the hands as they reach behind the hips toward the floor.
 c. Immediately sit and roll through the spine to lying position, while the arms slide along the floor to extend overhead and the legs are straight.

Backward Fall Through Hinge Position

Starting position: Begin by standing in parallel second position, arms down at sides.

Movement sequence:
 a. Execute a side body wave moving right to left.
 b. Back-circle the right arm down and up to front to finish in cut position at the ribs with torso contraction. The left arm remains in second.
 c. Begin a reverse windmill, starting with the right arm and finishing with the arms in opposition: left arm middle front, right arm middle back, slight torso twist to right. At the beginning of the windmill, straighten the legs and relevé. At the end of the windmill, remain in relevé but bend the knees so that the knees, the hips, and the shoulders are on one plane—the hinge position.
 d. Begin to lower the body toward the floor by bending the knees and maintaining the backward tilt position. As the knees touch the floor, support the body with the right hand.
 e. Lift your midsection and rotate the shoulder so that you are in a back bend position. Twist to the right, placing the left hand in front of you on the floor. Now slide the right arm out and straighten the legs until you are in a lying position. Roll onto the stomach.

Circular Fall From Low Inside Fan Kick

Starting position: Open the arms to second position and step forward onto the left leg in plié. Immediately lift the right leg to the side at 90-degree height and with a bent base leg.

Movement sequence:
 a. Cross the right leg over the left, stepping down onto the right foot, so that both knees are bent. Meanwhile, be pivoting to the left while lowering your body weight to the floor to rest gently onto the left knee. Continue with spiraling motion so that the right knee moves to the left knee, and the left foot joins the right foot.
 b. Flex at the hips so that you can sit just right of the legs. Remain sitting while you lift the knees toward the ceiling, keeping pointed toes on floor.
 c. Drop the legs to the left side of the body. Open to fourth sitting position while you twist the torso as far to the left as possible so that its support is on the left elbow. Allow the head to drop back, have the chest lift and arch, and sweep the right arm beside the torso and up overhead to high fifth position.

Circular Fall From Side Lunge

Starting position: Begin in parallel first position. Step to side lunge with the right foot and open the arms to the sides while the torso twists right into middle fourth position.

Movement sequence:
   a. Shift your weight to a left side lunge and twist the torso to the left.
   b. Take your weight all the way over onto the left leg. Begin to lower the left knee farther while twisting the hips left so that the right thigh folds into the left leg.
   c. Continue twisting left. Simultaneously lower the body to the floor until the weight rests on the right hip.
   d. Pivot on the hips to the left until the legs and knees come together. The feet are pointed, the tips of the toes resting on the floor.
   e. Continue pivoting on the hips to the left until the legs are in the sitting fourth position.
   f. Continue twisting the torso to the left. Meanwhile, reach as far behind as possible with the left hand. Slide the hand out until the body is lying on the floor in a curved C position.

Side Fall

Starting position: Stand on the right leg, the left leg pointed back, the arms in high parallel fifth position.

Movement sequence:
   a. Lower the body weight down to rest on the left knee.
   b. Sit onto the left hip and simultaneously place the left hand to the floor beside the left hip.
   c. Slide the left hand along the floor until the entire body is in a side-lying position with the legs straight.

Summary

Understanding and applying correct body placement is critical to the development of sound dance technique. Once this is achieved, the ability to maintain correct placement during the performance of all dance movements should be strived for. The gymnast who becomes acquainted with the basic principles of dance will be able to apply them not only to the execution of specific dance skills but also to many other areas of gymnastics.

The specific elements of dance that are discussed in this chapter are important not only for their individual application but also, on a broader scale, for their relationship to all other dance steps and movements. *Plié*, for example, is the beginning and ending of all movements of elevation. *Tendues* are important in the development of strong feet and well-turned legs as well as being a position that must be passed through during the execution of many other dance steps. The correct body positions that have been detailed here should be applied to the execution of steps throughout this book.

CHAPTER 3

Dance Patterns for Workouts

In the previous chapters, ways of incorporating dance into the workout schedule have been suggested, such as using the rotation method instead of separate dance sessions. Some very specific teaching goals regarding dance material have also been identified: instructing the gymnast in (a) fundamental dance technique, (b) exploration of dance skills and movement combinations, and (c) developing performance quality in all execution of dance movements. In chapter 2, some specific dance skills, styles, and techniques were explained. Now this chapter, with this information in mind, offers some suggestions and discussion on class content for the gymnast.

Incorporating Dance Elements Into the Workout

Regardless of whether dance elements are to be taught in separate dance sessions or integrated into the general workout schedule, there are several effective methods for presenting dance material. These methods may be used independently or collectively, depending on your program's individual needs and workout schedule. Keep in mind that all dance sessions should include (a) a warm-up; (b) exercises that stress correct technique and conditioning of appropriate muscle groups, and that feature movement phrases that develop locomotor skills, coordination, rhythm, fluidity, presentation, and the smooth integration of dance and gymnastic skills; and (c) a cooling-down period that emphasizes muscle-stretching and breathing exercises that relax the body.

Circle Practice

Your gymnasts could form a large circle and perform individual dance skills to music either in place or while moving in the circle. There are several advantages to this approach. First, the gymnasts' interest and enthusiasm easily surfaces because there is a sense of camaraderie in working together in this fashion. There is less opportunity for boredom and greater aerobic benefit because a well-planned session can keep gymnasts motivated and moving for a lengthy period of time. Also, it is very easy for you to observe the individual gymnasts and offer help where needed.

The circle practice can be prechoreographed for working on specific movements that need emphasis. Remember that a prechoreographed circle routine should include all of the previously discussed general aspects of a dance session. However, the specific elements can change from class to class for variety. The circle practice may be used either for the duration of a dance session or for only a portion of the class, for example, to warm up the locomotor skills.

Following are steps and movement combinations that can be included in the circle practice:

1. Walking brushes help develop strength in the feet, they work with turn-out of the legs.
2. Walking *grand battements* (grahn baht-MAHN) are high leg kicks to the front, the side, or the back while traveling.
3. *Chassés* (shah-SAY) are gliding steps where one foot literally chases the other. Variety can be added by
   - altering from side to side;
   - adding different *ports de bra* movements; or
   - alternating and adding a turn (*chassé* right, *chassé* left, *chassé* right turning, *chassé* left; repeat to the other side).
4. *Balancés* can move your gymnasts from side to side while they face into the circle.
5. Waltz steps can be used
   - turning (two waltzes to each rotation);
   - alternating while traveling forward, as in a triplet (down in bent knee, up in *relevé*, and up in *relevé* right, left, right); or

- in and away (facing into the circle, reaching up with one arm while waltz is in, and down and back with the same arm while waltz is away).
6. Step hops can be
   - alternating from side to side with leg in parallel *passé* (the arms swing side to side across the front of the torso);
   - alternating with straight leg lifted to front (the arms swing front and back in opposition);
   - combined with a turn hop in the air (step hop right, step hop left, step hop right, and turn in the air);
   - alternating with one leg in front *attitude*, raised to the front in a bent, turned-out position (the arms swing front and back in opposition); or
   - combined with a double stag (one leg raised to front *attitude*, base leg tucked under on hop while the arms swing front and back in opposition).

Drills that enhance endurance and strength can also be quite effective when used during circle work. Your gymnasts stand facing the middle of the circle and perform the following while moving from right to left along the path of the circle:

- Traveling to the right, they run right, run left, and make a small leap onto right run.
- They immediately change directions, traveling to the left, and repeat run, run, leap.
- They repeat the leap pattern once more to the right, still traveling along the path of the circle.
- They immediately follow this last movement with two preparatory steps left, then right, for a *saut de basque* (soh duh BAHSK) turn to the right (a traveling step in which the body turns in the air as the first leg brushes out and the opposite foot is drawn up to the knee of the first leg). When your gymnasts take the step onto the right foot, they immediately brush the left forward and push off the floor with the right. They rotate to the right, completing the turn in the air with the right leg raised into *passé* position (leg bent, toe at the left knee). They land onto the left foot in *demi-plié*.

Note that the directional changes are quick and the split leaps emphasize height and speed. Drills like this one are great fun for gymnasts and help break up the monotony of dance training. What's more important, they improve coordination, endurance, speed, and the understanding of weight transference. This kind of combination is also excellent because it takes dance movements out of the realm of isolated skills or tricks and places the emphasis instead on continuity, flow, and rhythm, teaching your gymnasts to move smoothly from one step to another.

Ballet Barre Work

This is usually less appealing for gymnasts because they tend to find the tedious repetition of standard ballet movements and the restriction of mobility irrelevant and boring. The easiest ways to overcome this are the following:

a. Avoid a standard or set barre routine that can be performed as though on automatic pilot. The gymnasts tend to lose focus, daydreaming instead of concentrating on correct technique and body alignment, diminishing the benefits of the barre work.

b. Incorporate a great deal of arm (*port de bra*) and upper torso work that can accompany the ballet work. Placing emphasis on presentation while encouraging the gymnasts to embellish their movements will help them benefit from and, at the same time, enjoy the practice.

c. Stimulate their intellectual understanding by explaining how the technique transfers to skills they need to perform. For instance, the amount of torso strength necessary to hold correct body placement helps ensure a more secure *pirouette*.

d. Generate enthusiasm in the gymnasts by conducting a class that is interesting and enjoyable.

A word of caution is needed with regard to ballet barre work and very young gymnasts. The goal of a classically trained dancer is to achieve a turn-out of 180 degrees, which is carefully developed and acquired over a period of several years. All ballet movements are based on this 180-degree turn-out. Therefore, the purpose of barre work is not only to warm up and condition the body but also to develop the technical understanding and ability to achieve and hold this purely classical position. Within the dance community, classes where ballet technique is stressed do not begin before the age of eight, with earlier training restricted to preballet or creative movement classes. This is because it is believed by dance professionals that prior to age eight the general musculature of the body is not yet developed to the point where it can withstand the stress of a purely classical position. Consequently, the potential for damaging the body would be greater for dancers or gymnasts who are too young.

Here are the dance steps that should be included in a ballet barre:

1. *demi-plié*
2. *pointe tendu*
3. *degagé*
4. *rond de jamb*
5. *développé*
6. *grand battement*

Movements Along a Straight-Line Path

After completing work at the barre, the gymnast can begin working skills that travel across the floor in a straight line. These should include the individual dance skills that are used frequently by the gymnast:

- *split leaps*
- *tour jeté*
- *pirouettes*
- *sissonne*
- *fouetté*

These can be worked successively, as in

run, run, leap; run, run, leap; run, run, leap.

Combinations are also effective, such as

- run, run, leap;
- step *tour jeté* with half-turn; and
- step close to fifth position *plié* and *sissonne*.

Combinations such as these will help the gymnast begin putting the movements together in a dance-like fashion. Emphasis should be placed on facial expression, exactness of arm and leg position, and upper body carriage.

Prechoreographed Routines

These can be very effective and enjoyable for the gymnast because they allow the elements of a ballet barre to be combined with other styles of movement in a less strictly classical fashion. Your gymnasts could stand together in a group and perform a set of prechoreographed movements that include various styles. They can be performed to contemporary music that may offer more appeal to the gymnasts.

Here are some of the elements that can be worked in a prechoreographed routine:

1. *Pliés* and *tendus* combined with *port de bras*

Example:

- One *plié* in first position (4 counts).
- Lift the arms through first, high fifth, and second position for the *port de bras* (4 counts).
- Cross the right foot directly behind the left; unwind to the right, straightening the legs and rising into *relevé* to finish facing front, with feet in parallel first (4 counts).
- Make a forward body wave with figure-eight arms (4 counts).

2. Leg brushes as well as *développés* and *rond de jambes* combined with arm swings, torso twists, body waves, and *balancés*
3. Jazz isolations, such as of the head, shoulders, ribs, and torso
4. *Pirouettes* and falls

Example:

- Do an outside *pirouette* on the left leg to the right; place the foot in fourth position back as you complete the turn (4 counts).
- Make circular, spiral *port de bras* with the arms and torso; the arms, shoulders, and head move to the right, back, left, and forward (4 counts).
- Swing the back leg forward and *fouetté* into *arabesque* (2 counts).
- With the right leg remaining in high *arabesque*, reach forward with both arms toward the floor and perform a chest fall, the right leg remaining lifted (2 counts).
- Extend the body and lie flat; roll to the left onto your back (1 count).
- Double straddle the legs, the right leg moving across and opening to side straddle as the left leg lifts to side straddle; finish by tucking both legs together as you push to rise up on the right hip, extending the left arm out and diagonally up to the back for pose (3 counts).

Summary

A good dance session should contain creative combinations that employ all styles of dance tempos, rhythms, and movements, which are then combined in a manner that is appropriate for floor and beam routines. Although aspects of traditional ballet technique are very important for the gymnast, classes that emphasize other styles and less structure in the composition of each particular step are the most fun for gymnasts. When dance movements are combined in creative and interesting ways, gymnasts not only find them less boring and repetitious, but more quickly learn to appreciate how relevant dance is to gymnastic performance.

PART II

Understanding the Choreographic Process

The choreographic process and the development of movement phrases are largely inspirational. Some people just seem to have a natural knack for creating interesting and visually appealing movement sequences. Others need to have a more intellectual understanding of the logical steps that go into choreography. This text will now analyze the basic elements that go into the art of choreography, both on the floor and the beam.

Chapter 4, "Understanding the Musical Elements," provides nuts-and-bolts explanations of the musical aspects of choreography, defining and illustrating basic musical terminology and rhythms. You are shown how these relate to dance movements that may be used during the choreographic process. Because this text refers to a number of different musical styles that are relevant to the gymnast, it may be helpful to familiarize yourself with the information in chapter 4 concerning the structure of corresponding musical styles.

The process of routine composition can be a very intimidating process for the novice choreographer. This is particularly true if one's dance experience and technical skills are limited. But, as with anything else, understanding is half the battle. Familiarizing oneself with the logical steps involved in the choreographic process will help give you a base to start from. Later, as you become more experienced, you will be able to expand on these ideas and develop your own techniques for composition.

Readers with less interest in the structural aspects of musical accompaniment should skip ahead to chapter 5, "Understanding the Movement." There movement qualities and methods of creating contrast in movement are described. These elements are necessary for lending texture and interest to the overall routine. Floor patterns are discussed in detail, and sample

© Dave Black

movement combinations are given to show how these different patterns might be used. Chapter 6 offers a step-by-step guide to where to begin and how to get started, which is followed by a "Choreography Checklist" for quick reference. In chapter 7 these same elements are identified for the purpose of beam composition.

CHAPTER 4

Understanding the Musical Elements

Musical accompaniment is required for all women's competitive floor exercise routines. Therefore, the ability to count music and hear varying rhythmic patterns is of primary concern for the choreographer during the compositional process. This ability can be a tremendous asset for the gymnast on beam as well when providing her own rhythmic variations to maintain an interesting performance.

The International Federation of Gymnastics (FIG) rules require that the gymnast move harmoniously with the music. To accomplish this, the gymnast must be musical, either able to "hear" and count the beats in the music, or possessing a natural sense of rhythm and timing. Without a natural sense of musicality, the gymnast will be unable to perform movements in time and in harmony with the music. While it may not be completely necessary for the gymnast, coach, or choreographer to have a basic understanding of music, time signatures, and notes and their values, it is certainly an advantage. Whether this understanding is intuitive or learned, the gymnast with it will give a more harmonious and fluid performance. Musical understanding can also help in adapting and applying rhythmic variations to any individual movement or movement phrase, thereby enhancing the gymnast's ability to interpret that music.

Time Signatures

All music fits into a basic time frame that is composed of measures and beats. The *beat* is the constant, underlying pulse in a piece of music, which falls at even and equal intervals throughout the piece (unless it is intentionally altered by the composer or the interpreter). This pulsing is similar to the steady beating of a heart or the constant drip of a water faucet.

The number of counts, or beats, each *measure* (a very short unit of the piece's division) is determined by the preceding *time signature*, two stacked numbers on sheet music, separated by a slash mark in text. Time signature may be indicated as 4/4, probably the most common to the gymnast; 3/4, generally a waltz; 2/4, a march; 6/8, which can also be used for marches and some folk dances; and many others. The first, top number in the time signature always tells us how many total beats there are in one measure. The bottom number tells what type of note will get one beat. So, with a 4/4 time signature ("in 4/4 time"), the total number of beats per measure is four, and a quarter note gets one beat. In 3/4 time, there are three beats per measure with a quarter note getting one beat; in 2/4 time, there are two beats per measure with a quarter note getting one beat; and in 6/8 time, there are six beats per measure with an eighth note getting one beat.

Time Value of Notes

Written musical notes are symbols that show how a time signature distributes its rhythm through a musical phrase. In combination with a given time signature, these notes have certain "time values." Remember that in a 4/4 time signature, there can only be 4 beats to one measure, and the second or bottom number in the time signature tells us which kind of note gets one beat. So in Figure 4.1, the musical symbol for a quarter note (a quarter of this measure) represents one beat. An eighth note, as seen in Figure 4.2, is equal to half of a beat. Figure 4.3 illustrates a half note, which is equal to two full beats; Figure 4.4 shows a whole note, which is equal to 4 full beats, the whole measure.

Figure 4.1. A quarter note in 4/4 time.

Figure 4.2. Two ways of showing an eighth note in 4/4 time.

Figure 4.3. A half note in 4/4 time.

Figure 4.4. A whole note in 4/4 time.

So, a 4/4 time signature tells us that there are four counts to one measure, with a quarter note getting one beat. A 3/4 time signature has only three beats to a measure, and a 2/4 time signature, two beats, with each time signature giving the quarter note one beat. If the time signature were instead 6/8, there would be six counts to a measure, and an eighth note would get one beat.

A dot (.) indicates that one-half again the value of the preceding note is added to its total value. In a 4/4 time signature, a dotted quarter note, written as shown in Figure 4.5, would receive one-and-a-half beats.

Pauses or rests in music are also indicated by symbols. Figure 4.6 shows a quarter rest, indicating a pause equal to one beat.

Rhythm

Rhythm is defined as any kind of movement characterized by the regular recurrence of strong and weak

Figure 4.5. A dotted quarter note in 4/4 time.

Figure 4.6. A quarter rest in 4/4 time.

elements in music. It is a series of pulsations that may be even or uneven. Any combination of notes and time values may be put together as long as they do not exceed the number of counts per measure indicated in the signature. In a 6/8 time signature, we might have six eighth notes (see Figure 4.7), with each of them getting one beat, so that the total number of beats in the measure would be six. We could mix eighth and quarter notes so that the total would still be six beats in the measure, such as using four eighth notes and one quarter note (see Figure 4.8). When notes of different values are combined into one measure, as in the previous example, we have a rhythm pattern. In a 4/4 time signature, for example, notes with time values greater or less than a quarter note are used to indicate rhythmic patterns and variations within the music.

Eighth notes are exactly one-half the value of quarter notes, when one appears alone, it is counted as "and." So, in a 4/4 time signature, four pairs of

Figure 4.7. Eighth notes in 6/8 time.

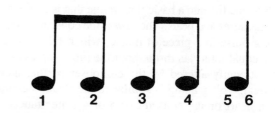

Figure 4.8. Eighth notes and a quarter note in 6/8 time.

eighth notes in a measure (see Figure 4.9) would be counted as "1-and 2-and 3-and 4-and." In a 3/4 time signature, we could not have more than three pairs of eighth notes per measure (see Figure 4.10). In a 2/4 time signature, we could have only two pairs (see Figure 4.11). Mixing eighth notes with notes of other values creates rhythm.

Figure 4.12 is an example of how a rhythmic pattern would be written using musical symbols. These four measures of notes represent one phrase of music, one rhythmic pattern. For the gymnast, a phrase is equal to one "sequence" of movement. Figure 4.13 shows how this same rhythmic pattern is counted.

Regardless of the number of notes that appear within each measure, all measures following a given time signature are equal in time, that is, they take the same amount of time to complete. In Figure 4.12 the second measure, which contains six notes, takes the same

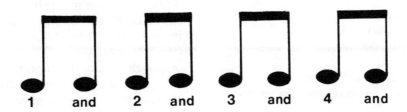

Figure 4.9. Counts per eighth note in 4/4 time.

Figure 4.10. Counts per eighth note in 3/4 time.

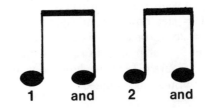

Figure 4.11. Counts per eighth note in 2/4 time.

Figure 4.12. One phrase of music in 4/4 time.

Figure 4.13. Sample counts per measure for one phase of music.

length of time to complete as the first measure, which contains only four notes, and as the last measure, which contains only two notes.

If we wanted to compose a movement sequence where one movement equals one beat exactly as shown in Figure 4.12, then a sample movement sequence could be this:

Measure one (four notes)
    Walk: RLRL
Measure two (six notes)
    Chassé (RLR); *Chassé* (LRL)
Measure three (four notes)
    Walk: RLRL
Measure four (two notes, two rests)
    Step on right foot and pose; step on left foot and pose

If this phrase were written instead in a 3/4 time signature, like that of a waltz, the first four steps could be changed to three steps, which in turn could be performed as a waltz step or a triplet traveling forward (Count 1 = step down on the right foot into *plié*; Count 2 = step up onto *relevé* with a straight left leg; and Count 3 = step up onto *relevé* with a straight right leg). Figure 4.14 shows how the waltz phrase would be written and counted.

Accents

A musical *accent* occurs when more emphasis is given to a particular note or notes within a given phrase. The accented beat or beats in the phrase appear to be heavier than the others, seeming to be played more forcefully. Accents are indicated by placing an accent symbol ($>$) under the notes that are to be emphasized.

For example, the phrase in Figure 4.15 shows accents on Count 1 in the first measure, Counts 1 and 4 in the third measure, and Count 3 in the second and fourth measures.

Although it is true that the time signature indicates how a piece of music is to be counted, the listener often determines the style of music by hearing and recognizing an identifiable rhythm. For example, although a polonaise, a mazurka, and a waltz all have 3/4 time signatures, they have different rhythm patterns and accents.

Waltz

In a traditional waltz pattern, the accent appears on the first beat of the measure and implies a heaviness to the first note of each *bar* (measure) (see Figure 4.16).

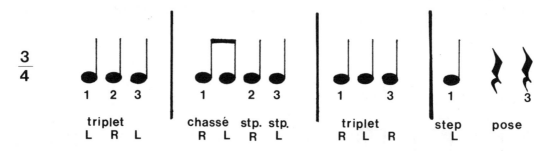

Figure 4.14. A sample movement phrase in 3/4 time.

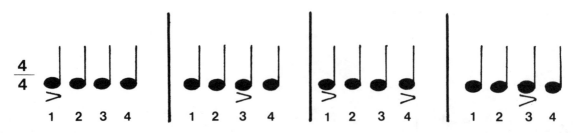

Figure 4.15. Various ways to accent within 4/4 time.

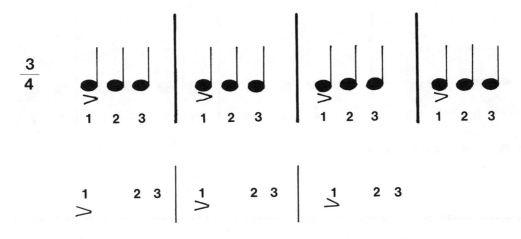

Figure 4.16. Typical waltz accents and counts.

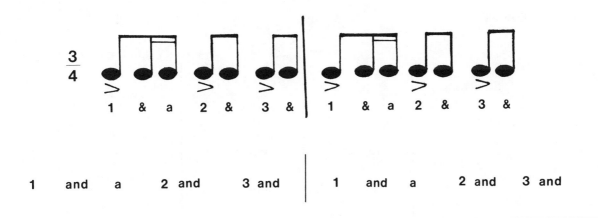

Figure 4.17. Typical polonaise accents and counts.

Polonaise

Polonaise is a stately, march-like Polish dance in triple time. Accents in a polonaise, as illustrated in Figure 4.17 are on Counts 1, 2, and 3—all three. Although a polonaise is in 3/4, it has a march feeling.

Mazurka

The illustration of the mazurka rhythm (Figure 4.18) shows the accents on the first beat in each of the first three measures and on the first two beats of the last

measure. So in the last measure both notes are accented to complete the rhythmic pattern of the phrase. You can see that the rhythm of a mazurka is much more lyrical than is that of a polonaise. Choreographically, either of these is more complex and interesting than a simple waltz. This is all accomplished through rhythmic variation.

Now let's look at how we might add movement to one of these rhythmic patterns. Figure 4.19 shows how both movement and counts might be added to a mazurka rhythm.

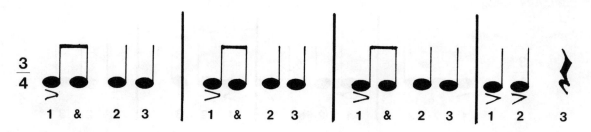

Figure 4.18. Typical mazurka accents.

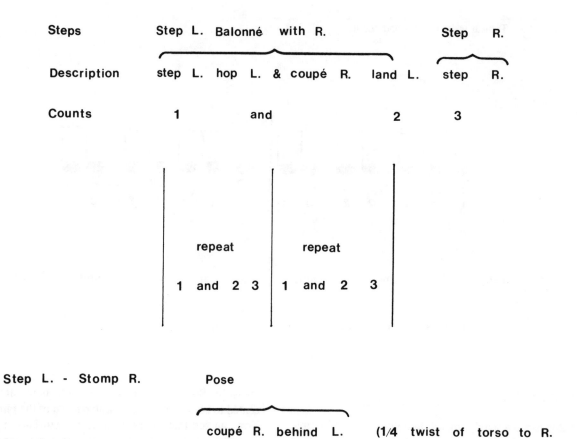

a

(cont.)

Figure 4.19. Two different movement phrases for mazurka rhythm.

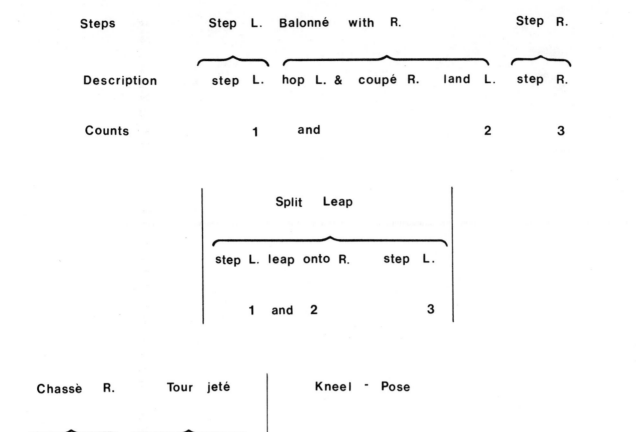

Steps	Step L.	Balonné with R.			Step R.
Description	step L.	hop L. & coupé R.	land L.	step R.
Counts	1	and	2	3

Split Leap

step L. leap onto R.   step L.

1   and   2   3

Chassè R.   Tour jeté

step R.L.R.   kick L.   land L.

1 and 2   3

b

Kneel - Pose

step back with R. and kneel onto L.   lean back onto L arm and extend R. leg 90° in air

1   2   3

Figure 4.19. (Continued).

Summary

A wide variety of musical styles are available when choosing musical accompaniment for a floor routine. These styles are often discernible by the various rhythms and accents expressed in the music. Becoming acquainted with the musical terminology that determines time signatures and note values, as well as becoming familiar with how music is counted, increases one's ability to create visually appealing movements. These movements can then complement any musical accompaniment chosen.

CHAPTER 5

Understanding the Movement

Movement—it is both conscious and unconscious; it is carefree or carefully directed; it is natural and personal, yet universal in its forms of expression. In daily life, movement is functional in activities such as walking or working. In the arts, movement is directed action for the purpose of creating images, making sounds, or communicating ideas. In no other art form is movement more basic to expression, and in no other art form is the body more an instrument of movement, than in dance.

All movement has both form and content. *Form* may be thought of as the relationship of movements that compose a particular phrase, whereas *content* refers to the individual movement skills or steps within that phrase. The content of a choreographed movement phrase is pretty well determined by the gymnast's individual skill level, but how does one give form to make the phrase interesting, appealing, and relevant to the routine?

Methods for Creating Contrast

When describing movement, descriptions such as *strong*, *smooth*, and *soft* are all relative terms. It is only through the use of contrast that we can actually see and identify any particular character or quality in the movement. Contrast in movement occurs when the energy exerted either initiates, controls, or totally stops the movement.

One method of creating contrast is to alter, through exertion, the intensity of a movement. The degree of intensity may range from almost imperceptible tension to sudden bursts of energy. Strong movements, performed with great force and high energy, can create excitement, whereas smaller movements, those performed with less energy and with controlled intensity, produce more contained forms of expression. Either one of these may be used successfully as long as the level of intensity that is demonstrated matches both the movement and the music.

Contrast may also be created by accenting movements. This is usually accomplished by displaying greater force or energy in one part of a particular motion. Movements that are performed with irregular accents of varying intensity create interesting visual patterns, whereas movements of regular accents create more balanced and monotonous movement patterns. Constructive use of irregular accents in a floor routine can create excitement and visual interest that enhance the gymnast's performance.

Varying levels is yet another effective method for creating contrast. Movements that take the gymnast to the floor in kneeling, sitting, and lying positions, as well as those performed in a standing position and while in flight, must all be included in a routine. Performing movements that alternate quickly from one extreme to another can be useful in creating a contrasting effect.

Movement Quality

Movement quality is determined by how energy is used when movement occurs, combined with the method chosen for moving a particular area of the body through space, such as isolated movements of an arm or a leg, or movement of the entire body.

Swinging Movement

These are created by dropping, due to the force of gravity, a particular part of the body, gathering momentum to move it in an opposing arc, then dropping it again when gravity interrupts that flow. The length of the body part that is swinging and the point from which the movement initiates both affect the speed of the action. An arm or a leg obviously swings with more facility than does the torso. Swinging movements may be lyrical and mellow, or strong and forceful, and can be used in conjunction with a variety of steps.

Percussive Movement

When movement is interrupted with sudden stops and starts, it is *percussive*. Jabs of energy with marked accents can give a movement overtones of excitement or strength. This type of movement could be appropriate for strong and dramatic music, or it might be used with music of a jazzy quality.

Sustained Movement

Movement that flows with no obvious beginning or ending is *sustained*. It is unaccented and presents a smooth progression of directed energy. Sustained movement might be accompanied by dramatic or emotional music. Sustained movement can be very broad and quite expressive but certainly requires a gymnast with proficient dance skills whose strength is in performance. It is best used combined with a released motion to show contrast. For example, a sustained lift of the arm to a high position followed by a sudden relaxing of the elbow produces a contrasting release caused by gravity.

Suspended Movement

This occurs in movements of elevation and can be seen, for example, at the high point of a leap, where for an instant the gymnast appears to be held aloft in space. This is the kind of dramatic and powerful quality the gymnast should strive to display in all movements of elevation.

Vibratory Movement

When percussive movement is performed repetitively and in quick succession, it is known as *vibratory* movement. This can be used when the gymnast wants to create a certain effect, such as dramatic or humorous. For example, smooth movement interrupted by a sudden and jerky vibratory arm shake, then followed by a quick release and a sudden stop, could be used for interpreting a robot's malfunctioning.

Seldom are any of these movement qualities found in any one pure form. Usually a movement phrase shows a combination of several identifiable qualities.

Moreover, a particular style of movement and music may require a dominance of one of these qualities.

Spatial Awareness

Movement exists in space, which means that there is a potential for both position and dimension. *Position* refers to the gymnast's level with regard to the surrounding space. In other words, movement can exist with the gymnast on the floor surface; standing (encompassing low movement performed with bent knees to higher movement performed in *relevé*); or in the air, as in any movement of elevation. *Dimension* refers to the size and direction of the movement relative to the performer as well as the performing space.

Using Floor Patterns in a Routine

When composing a floor exercise routine, you must give consideration not only to the content of the routine with regard to dance skills, movement phrases, and acrobatic skills, but also to the paths of travel for any of these elements. A well-composed routine must make effective use of the entire floor exercise area. Inability to accomplish this according to FIG floor requirements will result in the gymnast's receiving up to as many as three specific deductions. These deductions for "monotony in the direction of movement" are for

- insufficient use of the floor area,
- predominance of straight-line directions, and
- lack of gymnastic or gymnastic-acrobatic passages covering a great distance.

The first deduction, insufficient use of the floor area, can be easily avoided during the choreographic process by drawing a floor diagram of the routine. The second and third deductions are avoided by acquainting oneself with all of the floor pattern options that might be used during composition.

Although there are a number of possible floor patterns, it is unlikely that all of them would be used in any single routine. Factors determining the use of a specific pattern will be based on the nature of the specific dance elements and combination of elements that are used.

Following are identified the floor pattern possibilities that might be used. In instances where it is less obvious how a movement phrase might accompany a particular floor pattern, a sample is given.

Straight Line Effect

This is any movement that progresses forward or backward along a straight line parallel to the mat's sides. Straight-line movement can be taken parallel to the floor exercise mat's edge to connect one corner to the other. For example, if one tumbling pass has been completed and the next pass is going to follow fairly soon, the gymnast may want to use a straight movement phrase to get to the adjacent corner for the start of that next tumbling pass (see Figure 5.1a). The straight-line movement may also cut through the center of the floor exercise mat (see Figure 5.1b). A straight-line pattern is always parallel to two of the four sides of the mat, regardless of its placement within the exercise area.

A right-angle pattern is a straight line, a 90-degree turn, and another straight line. A square, of course, consists of four straight lines joined at four 90-degree corners all of which turn the same direction. Although these floor patterns might be used successfully to cover a certain area of the floor mat, keep in mind that they are still straight lines and could possibly seem overused to a judge. More than likely, a deduction for using too many straight lines will be given, reflecting monotonic movements.

Diagonal Line Effect

Movement performed on a diagonal is forceful and appears to "cut" through the space (see Figure 5.2). This formation should probably not be used for dance elements but should be reserved for the tumbling passes that typically travel from one corner to the opposite corner.

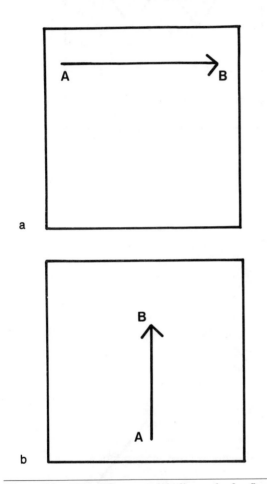

Figure 5.1.   Two different straight-line paths for floor exercise.

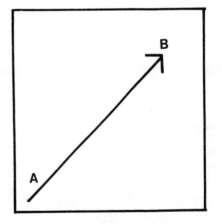

Figure 5.2.   A sample diagonal-line path

Zigzag Effect

This movement pattern combines diagonal lines in alternating direction, giving the movement a jabbing appearance. Zigzag formations are more appropriate for jazzy or dramatic music and movement. Keep in mind, however, that a zigzag pattern is not necessarily right for every movement, even one that is part of an appropriate general style (see Figures 5.3a and b).

Example 5.1 describes how a movement phrase might be performed in a zigzag pattern.

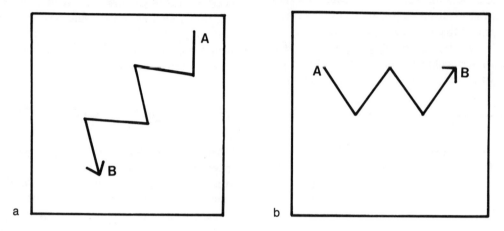

Figure 5.3. Two different zig-zag-line paths.

Example 5.1

Sample Combination for a Zigzag Floor Pattern

Movement Phrase

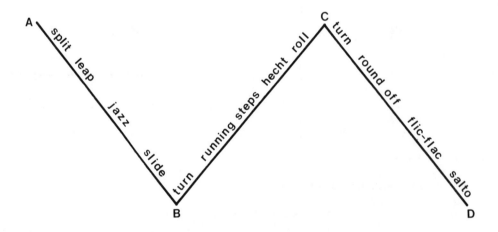

Beginning at point A and traveling to point B

1. Step left, split leap right. Swing arms in opposition on preparation step, then lift into left arm middle front, right arm middle side and diagonally back and up at 45 degrees. Keep focus with head and chest lifted on split leap.
2. Step left, forward jazz slide on left. Arms are in opposition to feet, with right arm forward, left arm back and diagonally down. Right leg is above 90 degrees.

Focus and chest are well lifted. Recover from jazz slide, transferring weight onto right foot.

At point B traveling to point C

3. Step forward on left, outside turn to right a 3/4 turn (270 degrees); left leg straight, right leg in *coupé* front position and turned. Right elbow is raised and bent with hand under chin. Left hand is diagonally down to side and straight. There is a strong lift in the upper back. The head is turned so that focus is toward left hand.
4. At finish of turn, immediately extend right leg to *arabesque allongée* with *plié*. Arms are parallel high fifth. There will be a straight arch in the body. Head is held in line with arm, and focus is down.
5. Travel backward with 3 running steps toward point C, 1 full twist to hecht roll. Arms are optional. Backward run is taken turning, so that as you take the 3rd step, you are facing point C.

At point C and traveling to point D

6. Three-fourths outside turn on left, stepping immediately onto round-off, flic-flac, salto backward stretched with half-twist (180 degrees). Arms are optional. On turn, spot direction where turn finishes.

Skill Difficulty Levels in This Example	
Split leap	A
Turn to balance element	B
Twist to hecht roll	B
Round-off, flic-flac, salto half twist	B

Semicircle Effect

These are half-circles that are connected to form an S pattern (see Figure 5.4). Semicircles lend themselves well to music that is smooth or lyrical. When used in combination with each other, they can exaggerate points of beginning and ending.

Example 5.2 is a sample of how a movement phrase might be performed in a semicircular floor pattern.

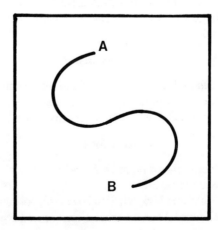

Figure 5.4. A joining of two semicircles creates a new path.

Example 5.2

Sample Combination for an S Floor Pattern

Movement Phrase

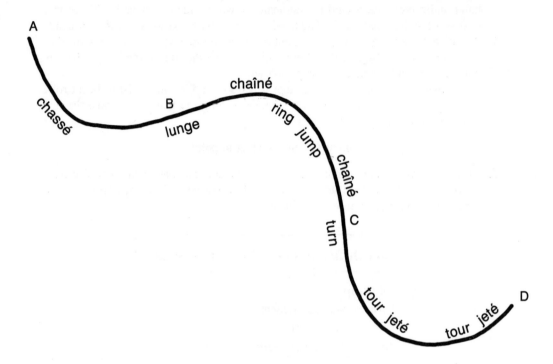

Beginning at point A and traveling to point B

1. Step forward on the right and execute 2 full inside turns with left leg elevated to side. Left arm is held in front middle position. Right arm is held in high fifth. Elevated leg must be straight and held at 90 degrees throughout turn. Arms are rounded. Turn is on right leg to left.
2. Form an inside half-circle by executing *chassés* (LRL, RLR).

At point B

3. Step on left with side lunge. Left arm is at side. Right arm moves in full circle lasso; focus is left, toward the left hand as lasso movement finishes with right hand over left hand.

Traveling point C

4. Following curve, *chaîné* turn to right (RL) and immediately bend knees to spring into ring jump. Land on right, step forward onto left, and perform 2 *chaînés* (RLRL). Arms in overhead V position on ring jump.

At point C

5. Step on right and focus toward point D. *Développé* and high-kick left leg to front. Arms in straight second position.
6. Step on left, then right and kick left into *tour jeté*, followed by another *tour jeté* with additional 1/2-turn. Arms overhead and open to second.

Skill Difficulty Levels in This Sample	
Double turn	C
Ring jump	B
Tour jeté	B
Tour jeté, 1/2 turn	B to C

Scallop Effect

Scallops are consecutive half-circles looping the same direction. They may be effective for exaggerating points of beginning and ending (see Figure 5.5).

Example 5.3 is a sample of how a movement phrase might be performed in a scallop floor pattern.

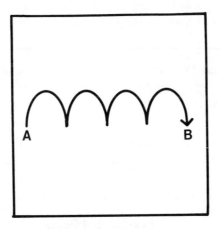

Figure 5.5.   Consecutive semicircles creates a new path.

Example 5.3

Sample Combination for a Scallop Floor Pattern

Movement Phrase

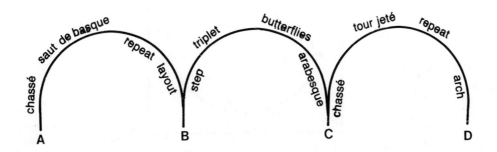

Beginning at point A and traveling to point B

1. *Chassé* (RLR) and *saut de basque* turn to right, landing on left leg. Repeat *saut de basque* turn by stepping on right and landing on left leg. Arms straight second position. Be sure to "spot" on *saut de basque* turn.
2. Step forward on right and execute round off, backward layout. Arms in V position over head on landing.

At point B traveling to point C

3. Step on left and travel forward with triplet runs (RLR) and two butterflies. Arms held straight side on triplet. Preparation for butterflies is on left leg for takeoff.
4. At point C, out of butterfly stepping on left, then step onto right leg for *arabesque allongé* and *plié* on base leg. Arms in high parallel fifth position.

At point C and traveling to point D

5. *Chassé* (LRL), step onto right and brush left leg forward into a *tour jeté*. Repeat *tour jeté* with additional 1/2-turn. Arms straight side throughout.

At point D

6. Step forward on right and lift leg to parallel *passé* with upper back arch. Arms diagonally down and back. Balance in parallel *passé* arched position.

Skill Difficulty Levels in This Sample	
2 butterflies	B
Tour jeté	B
Tour jeté, 1/2 turn	B to C

Circle Effect

This is the most complete of curved lines. A circle is an excellent pattern to use for fulfilling the requirements of a gymnastic or gymnastic-acrobatic phrase that must cover a large, sweeping area (see Figure 5.6).

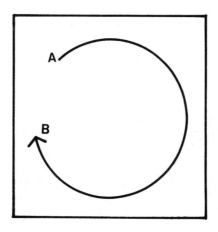

Figure 5.6.   A sample curved path.

Figure Eight Effect

A figure eight pattern is created when a circle is doubled in the opposite direction (see Figure 5.7). A sample movement combination for a figure eight floor pattern is also provided in Example 5.4.

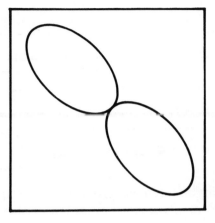

Figure 5.7.   A double circle creates a figure eight pattern.

Example 5.4

Sample Combination for a Figure Eight Floor Pattern

Movement Phrase

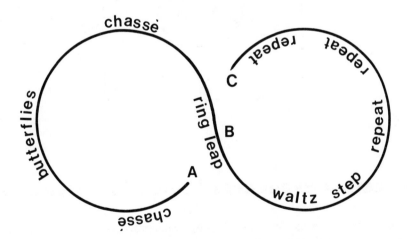

Beginning at point A and traveling to point B

1. *Chassé* (LRL), step forward to face into the circle for two butterflies with right leg. On *chassé* arms begin left and move across and down to right (parallel figure eight).
2. *Chassé* (RLR) and step on left. Left arm front middle, right arm side middle.

At point B

3. Ring leap with right. Arms high fifth position. Landing from leap is on the right foot, followed immediately with a forward step onto the left.

Traveling point C

4. Four waltz steps turning (RLR, LRL, RLR, LRL). On first waltz, right arm straight high fifth position with palm facing out and left arm straight middle. On second waltz, left arm remains side, right arm scoops down and up to first position. Repeat same arms on third and fourth waltzes. When arm is to straight middle position, palm faces down.

Skill Difficulty Levels in This Sample	
2 butterflies	B
Ring leap	B

Spiral Effect

Spirals are also excellent for fulfilling the requirements of gymnastic or acrobatic-gymnastic combinations that cover a large, sweeping area. Spirals may become either larger or smaller as they gather speed and momentum (see Figure 5.8).

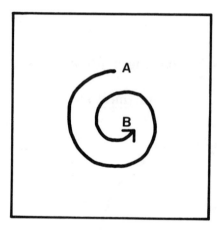

Figure 5.8. A sample spiral pattern.

Creating Sequences From Floor Patterns

Understanding and using floor patterns during the choreographic process can also be helpful as a tool for giving rise to more creative and interesting element combinations or dance sequences. For example, say that you need to use a leap-acrobatic combination but can't think of anything creative or different. Instead of starting to plan the movement, the leap-acrobatic combination, try beginning with a floor pattern such as a spiral or a scallop. Think of different ways that you can put together a leap-acrobatic combination that will fit the floor pattern.

To help you see how changing your perspective can change a combination, make up a movement phrase for both of the following problems while using the same elements:

- Leap
- 1-1/2 to 2 full turns
- Salto forward tuck, straddle jump
- One or two connecting steps, such as *chassés*, runs, or skips

Problem A

Perform a movement combination using the preceding elements in any order on a straight-line path. Refer to Example 5.5 for a description and illustration of a possible solution.

Example 5.5

Possible Solution Using a Straight-Line Path

Movement Phrase

A	step L.		body wave step L hop	pirouettes	salto tuck B
chassé R. L. R.	split leap R.		step R. hop	turn in air	straddle jump

Beginning at point A and traveling to point B

1. *Chassé* (RLR), step left, split leap with right, landing on the right. Arms at side for the *chassé*. Left arm middle front and right arm middle side for leap.
2. Step on left, then bring right together to left in parallel first position for forward body wave to backward scale (left leg is extended forward). Figure eight arms for body wave, and move to overhead V for scale. Leg is above 90 degrees on scale and is forward, torso is inclined backward.
3. Recover from backward scale and step left and hop, step right and hop. Step forward on left and perform two outside turns to right, then step with right together to left and perform 1 full turn in air. Arms swing to left on left-hop and arms swing to right on right-hop. Right foot to *coupé* back position on hop. Left foot to *coupé* back on hop to right.
4. Salto forward tuck, straddle jump.

Problem B

Perform a movement combination using the preceding elements in any order in an S pattern. Refer to Example 5.6 for a description and an illustration of a possible solution.

Example 5.6

Possible Solution Using a Semicircular Pattern

Movement Phrase

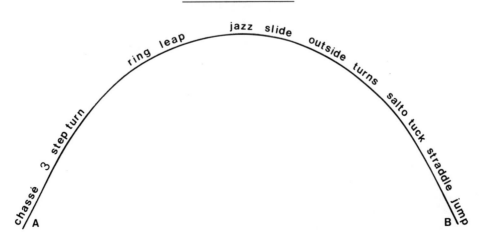

Beginning at point A and traveling to point B

1. *Chassé* (LRL). Left arm side middle, right arm forward middle. Head focuses left on *chassé*.
2. Three-step turn to right (RLR). Arms straight side middle. In preparation for a leap, *plié* on the last step of the turn.
3. Step on left, ring leap with right. Arms high fifth position.
4. Step forward on left and jazz slide to right. Right arm side middle, left arm forward middle.
5. Transfer weight onto right foot after jazz slide, and then cross left over right and outside double turn on left.
6. Step on right and bring left to right for salto forward tuck, straddle jump. Arms optional on straddle jump.

Summary

Individual movements that are performed evenly and with no highs or lows are monotonous. This can be prevented by performing movements that reflect swinging, percussive, sustained, vibratory, or suspended qualities. Entire movement phrases can be altered to show contrast as well. These phrases may then be performed in a variety of floor patterns that lend interest and appeal to the final routine.

CHAPTER 6

Choreographing Floor Routines

Although composing a routine depends heavily on one's intuitive and creative abilities, some basic steps can be followed when creating a floor exercise routine. This chapter identifies four steps to consider before beginning the compositional process, suggests ways to help you get started choreographing routines, and provides a detailed choreography checklist for you to use.

Step 1: Choosing the Music

The music for floor exercise accompaniment must be chosen before choreography can begin. A great deal of consideration should be given to this choice because the gymnast is likely to have to live with this music for one competitive season at the very least, if not longer. There are a number of points to consider when choosing music:

- The style of music must fit the gymnast's physical stature, level of capability, and personality. Dramatic, grand music is less appropriate for a youthful, petite, pixie-like gymnast than for a sophisticated, more mature gymnast.
- Try to stay away from popular movie themes, no matter how appealing. Choose instead more obscure musical pieces that can enhance the gymnast's individual style and personality. This reduces the risk of getting to competition and finding another gymnast performing to the same music. Apart from the obvious implications of such a situation, keep in mind that judges grow tired of hearing the same music over and over again and will certainly appreciate your originality.
- Avoid overly trite music that leaves little opportunity to be creative or original in the choice of movement.

- On the other hand, also avoid music with complicated musical phrasing unless the gymnast naturally possesses a strong sense of timing and musicality. Because this is not completely an area of understanding that can be taught, the gymnast with less musicality will meet with greater success when sticking to music that has a beat or rhythm that is strongly stated.
- Are there logical places in the music that will complement the tumbling passes (in the acrobatic series)?
- Are there sufficient musical contrasts and rhythmic changes to satisfy FIG requirements? Routines must contain both slow and fast movements that correspond to the music. To prevent monotony in movement, the music should offer some rhythmic variety.
- Is the introduction and the ending of the music appropriate for the movement you would like to give the gymnast? Does it inspire you? Is the gymnast comfortable with the tempo of the music? Is the music compatible with the gymnast's skill level? Very simple music with straightforward rhythmic patterns and simplistic musical phrasing is the best choice for a beginning-level gymnast. An advanced gymnast, however, needs music that is more intricate and that allows the use of complicated movement patterns that will better display gymnastic and rhythmic talents.
- Finally, the style of movement must complement the music that is chosen, that is, all movement must be in harmony with both the rhythm and character of the music, whether it be dramatic, gay, or even humorous. Certain musical choices, such as ragtime and folk, may automatically imply a particular style of movement.
- No matter what the musical choice, it should always be determined by the style of movement that the gymnast is most suited to performing.

For example, if the gymnast is more comfortable with lyrical, ballet-type movements, music with a jazzy flavor would be inappropriate.

For the majority of competitive gymnasts, the most suitable accompaniment for floor routines is commercially prepared music. Fortunately, there are available on the market a great many recordings specifically designed for gymnastic competition. These normally offer the gymnast a variety of styles to choose from and can accommodate various levels of abilities.

However, there may come a time when the more advanced gymnast may wish to use musical accompaniment prepared specifically for him or her. Naturally, this would give an opportunity to use music more closely fit to both the gymnast's personality and gymnastic style. It also guarantees the originality of the musical selection.

If an original composition is chosen, be certain that the selection complies with all FIG requirements. Keep in mind that musical accompaniment may be performed only by one of the following: full orchestra, piano accompaniment only, or accompaniment by another single instrument. Only piano accompaniment may be performed live during competition. Any other type of instrumentation must be prerecorded and played on tape. The musical accompaniment must be 70 to 90 seconds long.

Regardless of whether the musical accompaniment is original or commercially prepared, understanding how to choose the music for a routine will certainly help the novice choreographer in beginning the movement composition.

Step 2: Determining the Movement Style

Once the music has been chosen, the style of movement most appropriate for that musical choice can be determined. Consideration must be given to the flavor, the tone, and the rhythmic structure of the music. These indicate whether the movement style should be ballet, folk, jazz, modern, or character. Depending on your choice of music, the style of the movement may be fairly obvious. If the music is typically ethnic, the movement style will naturally be folk dance. If the music has a great deal of pizzazz, jazz dancing will probably serve best. In some cases, a contemporary or popular piece of music may not indicate one particular style over another. At such a time, it will be necessary for you to consider the movement style that is best suited to the gymnast's abilities, along with musical and theme considerations.

Step 3: Listing the Elements

Decide which tumbling sequences, acrobatic skills, and dance elements the gymnast is to use. There are some general thoughts on this to keep in mind:

- Make a list of individual acrobatic combinations or skills that you would like to put into the routine, such as walkover, a valdez (an extended tuck-sit position, backwards to a handstand), and so on.
- Decide on any particular dance elements that you would like to use and make a list. For example, do you wish to use a stag leap or a switch-leg leap? Do you have a leap combination in mind? What type of turn would you like to include? Is there a dance element that your gymnast performs particularly well, such as *jeté*? If so, that should be noted.

Once these lists are complete, they will serve as your guide for creating the floor exercise routine. These lists are your constants and will help you remain focused.

Step 4: Developing the Theme

A *theme* is an underlying, identifiable thread that runs consistently throughout a composition. In a routine, this thread should be seen in some aspect in every movement throughout the entire routine. It should also be in keeping with the style of the musical accompaniment.

Keep all this in mind during the composition process so that every element performed by the gymnast is harmonious with the implied theme. Developing a theme through the choreography is one method of making sure that a routine has consistency and continuity of style: The movements make sense, have direction, and have focus. You should always avoid stringing together a conglomeration of movements that have no relationship to each other, to the gymnast, or to the music. Choreographically speaking, something must be used to tie the whole routine together. Giving the routine a theme can accomplish this.

Some areas of consideration when thinking about a theme are these:

- Mood of the music, implying appropriate sense of movement
- Rhythmic structure or variation of the music
- Style of music, such as folk, rock, or jazz

Creating a Mood

Let's say that the musical choice is one that creates a mood of strength. How might this be used to develop a theme?

Example:

Mood

Dramatic, bold, expressive, daring

Style of movement

Large, sweeping movements that show contrast, sudden changes in direction and levels, and so on; strong, sharp movements

If the theme in a routine is to be developed by the mood indicated in the music, the type of steps that are chosen—whether they be folk, ballet, jazz—will become secondary to the manner in which those steps are performed.

Let's consider a 3/4 time piece of music with a folk dance flavor. If it is particularly bright and quick in tempo, it might suggest a style of movement that is flirtatious, fun, and playful. This playful attitude would then prevail throughout the routine and could be used as the theme. The gymnast performing to this type of music should be quite facially expressive and employ movements that contribute to this playful attitude, not merely any movements of a folk dance nature. Naturally, a smaller gymnast with a pixie quality would be more suited to this type of interpretation.

On the other hand, if the music (folk dance style and in 3/4 time) were slower and heavier in nature, a more dramatic interpretation might be called for. Here an aloof and sophisticated quality might better serve these same folk dance movements. A kind of earthiness could be suggested in the quality of the movement through the execution of some deep lunges, punctuated with an air of sophistication. This style would be an appropriate choice for a gymnast with a more mature disposition.

Rhythmic Variation

Another way to determine the theme in your floor exercise routine might be to look within the rhythmic structure of the music. A particular movement or step that corresponds to the rhythm could be repeated throughout the routine, each time altered slightly to enhance the pattern.

Consider as an illustration the rhythmic pattern inherent in a mazurka. Because a mazurka is 3/4 time and has somewhat of a folk dance flavor, we will use it as our style choice here. A mazurka calls for dance steps that rely heavily on the use of shouldering and bent knees as well as such movements as stomps and hitch-kicks. Remember that a mazurka is played with an accent on the first beat of each measure, so movement may also be emphasized on that beat by larger steps or heavier movements.

The following is an example of a movement combination that could be performed to the rhythmic structure of a mazurka:

Begin the movement with the *ballonné*, a typical folk dance step. (*Ballonné* is performed by stepping on the left foot, hopping into the air and simultaneously brushing the right foot diagonally out to the side, before quickly bringing it back to *coupé* position at the left ankle as you land on the left leg.) Execute this movement with the hands on the hips and with a slight twist of the torso to the left while focusing out over the right shoulder.

Tempo

The *tempo* is the speed at which a piece of music is played. Though the tempo of a musical phrase must remain consistent within that particular phrase, it is not inappropriate for the gymnast to combine musical phrases of differing tempos within the total accompaniment of the floor routine. Indeed, it is necessary in fulfilling FIG rules for the gymnast to show both slow and fast movements. Although this can be accomplished by using a combination of various tempos (e.g., 3/4, 4/4, or 6/8 timing), it is not necessary. As long as the movement remains harmonious with the music, the tempo changes in the movement may or may not accompany an altered musical tempo.

Musical Style

Another method for developing a theme is simply to use the musical style, if possible. When style is used as the basis for determining a theme, the least complex factor making that determination will be found in the time signature of the music. A choice of music that strongly implies a specific style may in turn predetermine a certain type of movement. This particular type of movement or style of movement then becomes the theme for the floor routine.

In a 3/4 time folk polonaise, for example, the obvious choice of movements will be typical folk-style dance, with such steps as stomps, hitch-kicks, *pas de basques*, and the like, all executed with the appropriate arm accompaniment. Variations on a waltz step or triplet would also be appropriate. All of these movements would take on a folk dance feeling if performed with the hands on the hips and adding the use of shouldering to lend a coquettish flair. Any other movements that further enhance or develop a folk dance feeling would also be appropriate.

Using a theme as the basis for composition of a floor routine greatly enhances the quality of the routine for several reasons. It can serve as a focal point for you during the choreographic process. It can lend continuity and consistency to a routine and add depth to the performance. Remember that a good routine is not just 1 minute and 10 or 30 seconds of unrelated movement styles, steps, and gymnastic elements haphazardly strung together. Performing movement in harmony with the music means more than just synchronizing movement and music. Deciding on a theme for your floor exercise can help you accomplish this.

Structure and Composition of a Floor Routine

Once you have considered the basic stages of choreography, you are ready to begin the actual composition process of your floor routine. Rather than listening to an entire piece of music and wondering where to begin, try separating the piece into three logical sections.

Introduction

The length of the introduction in the routine is determined by the length of the opening segment of the musical accompaniment that you choose. During this portion of the music, the gymnast may either strike an opening pose that is held through the introduction or immediately begin movement that is choreographed to complement this portion of the music. Listen to the phrasing in the music to discover whether you can hear an opening segment that will serve as the introduction. Listening to the phrasing of the music should help you decide how long the introduction actually is. Although FIG rules allow the gymnast to take up to four measures of music before beginning movement, the musical introduction may be shorter or longer than this.

Generally speaking, the gymnast should use the musical introduction to introduce him- or herself and his or her style of movement to the audience. In particular, it is in the opening few moments of a routine that the judges get their first impressions of the gymnast. Although it is certainly possible to open the routine with a pose that is immediately followed by

the first tumbling pass, it should not be choreographed in this way unless the musical opening is explosive and dynamic, requiring complementary movement. Rather, in the opening moments of the routine, it is more effective to place emphasis on setting the mood for the rest of the performance. It is an excellent idea to choreograph a few dance poses or minor dance movements that give the judges a moment to get acclimated to the performer and how he or she moves.

Some indication of the type or style of movement that will follow should be evident during the introduction of the routine. When possible, this movement should in some way relate to the viewer, giving at least a hint of what is to come. The gymnast has an opportunity in the very beginning of the routine to convey something to the audience: (a) I'm going to be lyrical; (b) I'm going to be dramatic and emotional; or (c) I'm going to dazzle. Keep in mind that 1 minute and 10 seconds is a very brief period of time, so the gymnast must make a significant impression in the opening moments of the routine. Above all, the gymnast needs to show him- or herself off to the best advantage, give the audience a taste of what is to come, allow them a moment to digest it all, then lead them enthusiastically along when beginning the bulk of the routine.

Main Body

The middle, or *main body*, of the routine must contain all gymnastic and acrobatic requirements while remaining consistent and harmonious with both the music and the movement style that was established during the introduction. More than likely, all three of the required tumbling passes will be contained in the main body of the routine. The placement of the tumbling passes will be determined by your listening to the stylistic quality and phrasing of the music and matching music and passes accordingly. Be sure that the length of the musical phrase corresponds to the time it takes to complete the entire pass. As a general rule, it is safe to say that every tumbling pass should be completed close to the end of a musical phrase. Because the gymnast must execute a secure and poised landing from all tumbling passes, it is harmonious to finish in time with the musical punctuation or pause that usually follows a phrase.

Once you determine the placements and length of the tumbling passes, continue counting the music to calculate how much time there is between each pass. Then insert appropriate dance elements and required acrobatic skills to fill these spaces.

Closing

The final phrase of the music is used for the gymnast's dismount and final pose. The closing of the routine may be as simple as performing the last gymnastic pass and moving into the final pose, or it might be choreographically more complicated, such as a short dance sequence and acrobatic combination. Regardless of whether the routine finishes with a pose or a short movement combination, it must complement the musical phrasing. Keep in mind, also, that the finish of a routine is every bit as important as the beginning: It is the final impression that the judges are left with. The finish should leave an impression of clarity and confidence.

Starting Procedures

Here is a format that you may follow to help get started. Keep in mind that the order of the elements here is merely a general suggestion and that many other possibilities exist for choreographing a routine.

- The *opening pose* may be followed by a short dance phrase or series of poses, depending on what is musically implied. Keep in mind the endurance level of the gymnast: The opening should not include anything too physically challenging if the gymnast has a tendency to become fatigued early in the performance.
- The *first tumbling pass* should be followed by a short dance phrase or a dance-acrobatic combination.
- The *setup for the second tumbling pass* must begin from a different corner from the setup for the first tumbling pass.
- The *bulk of dance and artistic requirements* should cover as much of the floor area as possible. Near the end of this section, pacing is once again important: Something simple yet still attractive and interesting should be used.
- The *final tumbling pass* falls near the very end of the routine so that there is just enough time for one last, brief dance sequence before moving into the final pose.

When you have completed planning the routine, draw a diagram of the floor pattern. If there are areas that are overused, it is a simple matter to rectify without needing to make any major choreographic changes. Usually the problem can be solved by retaining the connecting dance or acrobatic elements and simply altering their direction.

Finally, fill out the choreographer's checklist at the end of this chapter and review your own list of desired skills, along with FIG's Code of Points, to be certain that you have not forgotten any necessary elements.

One final thought with regard to the placement of the tumbling passes: If either the introduction or the closing is musically very strong, it is not out of the question to begin or finish the routine with a tumbling pass. However, be certain that doing so is indicated by the music. Generally, though, it is more appealing to see the gymnast perform some movement both at the beginning of the routine (before actually starting the tumbling requirements) and at the end of the routine.

Summary

Before doing anything else, when choreographing a floor routine, decide on the musical accompaniment. Very little can be accomplished until this selection is made, and all parties concerned—gymnast, coach, and choreographer—must be happy with the choice. It is fairly obvious that the gymnast must be comfortable with the musical selection, but the person involved in the composition of the routine must also be comfortable with the final choice. If the music fails to inspire either of these individuals, the finished product will be less than satisfying.

Once the musical accompaniment is settled on, the style of movement that best fits this accompaniment can be determined. Then, before beginning any actual choreography, you should work out the tumbling passes and list all dance elements and acrobatic skills that are to be included in the routine. These then serve as the core from which all other aspects of the routine evolve. Following this, consideration can be given to theme development. Remember that the theme lends direction and purpose to movement phrases within the routine and also serves as a common thread that pulls all other pieces into one unified presentation. Selecting a theme ultimately helps avoid a hodgepodge routine composed of elements thrown together haphazardly, lacking flow and continuity—a potpourri of unrelated movements that falls between the various required elements of FIG competitive rules.

A well-choreographed routine develops logically, showing a natural progression of movements that make a statement of intent, add substance to the presentation, and arrive at a climactic finish. Even the best performer cannot fare well if the material does little to enhance his or her abilities.

Choreography Checklist for Floor

As soon as you begin to choreograph the routine, start to review the Choreography Checklist for Floor. Notice that there are four parts to the list. Across from each item is a blank space. As you fulfill a particular requirement, place a check mark (✔) in the space. If an item is not an element you are going to use in your routine, indicate this with an X.

As you begin the choreographic process, you may be uncertain about exactly how you will fulfill some of the FIG requirements that are included in the list. Leave the space opposite such items blank. As you continue to work on your routine, you can easily see which items still need to be included by reviewing the list. As you put each of the remaining required elements into the routine, be sure to go back to the list and mark off that particular item.

Part I lists all of the general aspects of the routine and refers to the structure. By the time the routine is completed, all items in this section should have been checked off.

Part II of the list indicates the various dance elements that might be included in a routine. Most of these should have been checked off by the time the routine is completed. However, the performance time limitation being what it is, you will have a few exceptions. For example, you probably will not include both a leap series and a singular leap (one used for emphasis or accent) in the routine unless you are absolutely certain it will enhance the performance of the gymnast.

Part III lists all possible floor pattern variations. When the routine is complete, draw a floor plot indicating the spacing and directions of all movements in the routine. Use a plastic-covered, square piece of white paper for this purpose. With a felt-tipped pen, draw a complete diagram of the routine. Adjustments and alterations can be made easily by wiping the plastic surface clean. Compare the floor diagram you have drawn to the Choreography Checklist for Floor; check off the floor patterns that you have used. Be certain that you have not relied too heavily on any one type of floor pattern.

Part IV covers general execution. This section of the checklist has less to do with the actual structure and content of the routine but is more concerned with the gymnast's performance and presentation. These items are to be checked off after the gymnast has completely learned the routine and performed all difficult elements successfully five times. For example, say you have included a *tour jeté*, which must be performed with straight legs, in the routine. If the gymnast has been having trouble with this movement, don't check off "Straight legs" until the gymnast has performed the *tour jeté* correctly in five practice routines in a row.

Directions: As you fulfill each requirement, place a check mark in the opposite space. Example: The music chosen is of appropriate length. Therefore, "Music 1:10 to 1:30 long ✔." If you are not going to use a particular element, indicate so with an X. *Example*: "Hops X ."

I. Content

In the FIG Code of Points, the term *gymnastic* refers to dance elements, and the term *acrobatic* refers to all tumbling elements.

When the routine is completed, all of the following elements should be checked off.

Music 1:10 to 1:30 _____

Three different acrobatic series, each with 3 acrobatic elements and 1 salto _____

One of the 3 acrobatic series to contain 2 saltos or 1 double salto _____

One gymnastic series of 3 elements (leaps, jumps, hops, or turns) _____

One gymnastic/acrobatic direct connection _____

Dismount, containing acrobatic or gymnastic element of B level _____

Beginning pose, setting mood and consistent with style of music and movement _____

Ending pose, making a statement such as dramatic, cute, or accented _____

Level changes—movements taking gymnast to the floor in lying, sitting, or kneeling position, as well as movements of elevation _____

Distribution of difficulty elements, spaced throughout the routine _____

Rhythmic variations and tempo changes _____

II. Dance (Gymnastic) Elements

Review the dance steps and consider ways they can be used to fulfill the following categories.

Turns: single ( ), double ( ), triple ( )   _____

Poses: standing ( ), sitting ( ), or lying ( ) positions   _____

Connecting steps   _____

Running combinations   _____

Movements of elevation   _____

   Singular leaps (as emphasis or accent)

   Leap series

   Hops

   Jumps

Arm swings   _____

Body waves   _____

III. Floor Patterns

Compare your diagram of the routine to this list of floor patterns and check off all patterns used in your routine. Be sure that your floor patterns create an even distribution of elements.

Straight line, movement progressing forward or backward along a straight line parallel to the outer edges of the floor exercise area   _____

Diagonal, movement appearing to ''cut'' through space traveling from corner to corner   _____

Zigzag, combining diagonals and giving movement a jabbing quality   _____

Circular   _____

Figure eight   _____

Spiral   _____

IV. General Execution

Fill in this section once the gymnast completely learns the routine. Use this section as a guide to help develop and polish the routine. Under ''Amplitude,'' do not check off an item (such as ''Straight legs'') unless the movement required is consistently performed with the legs straight.

Movement and music appropriate for gymnast   _____

Torso movements   _____

Expressive use of arms, head, and shoulders   _____

Each movement complete before next movement begins   _____

Smooth transitions between all movements and elements   _____

Amplitude   _____

   Pointed feet   _____

   Movements performed in high *relevé*   _____

   Straight legs   _____

   Good posture   _____

   Effective use of upper body   _____

   Good facial expression   _____

CHAPTER 7

Choreographing Beam Routines

The structure and the composition of balance beam routines are simplified by two factors: There is no musical accompaniment, and all movements must be performed on a straight-line path. Keeping that in mind, this chapter will examine which choreographic elements do relate to balance beam composition. The difficulty in choreographing for the balance beam is finding ways of making a routine stand out above the others. Everyone wants to perform a routine that will do more than just display one's skill level, but many people are not sure where to begin or how to accomplish this. In this chapter we will identify and look at other elements that go into making a routine unique and interesting.

The first area of consideration is the basic structure of the routine. Speaking in broad terms, this structure consists of all elements that are to be included in the routine, such as the mount, the dismount, acrobatic and dance skills, and so on. This portion of the composition is fairly simple because these elements are largely determined by the skill level of the gymnast as well as FIG requirements for competition.

Next come choosing a theme and deciding on a style of movement. Experimentation with these areas can be very useful and often give rise to inspirational movements that make one particular routine more interesting than another.

Movement methods that can be used to enhance the flavor of a routine and add the necessary variety required by FIG regulations will be identified. These include rhythmic variation, directional and level changes, and movement quality and contrast.

Finally, this chapter will examine what is involved in moving beyond the execution of skills to achieving dynamic presentation in a balance beam performance.

Structure

As stated earlier, because there is no musical accompaniment to contend with, the composition of a balance beam routine is a great deal easier than that of a floor routine. As with floor, the simplest place to begin is with a list. The following suggestions will help you compile your list:

- Decide what your gymnast's mount and dismount will be; note these.
- List any dance steps that your gymnast performs particularly well and would like to use, such as *tour jeté*, *assemblé* with a beat, *cabriole*, and so on.
- List all acrobatic skills you wish to include.
- Decide on any leaps to be used.
- Which turn or turns do you plan on using?
- Experiment with poses until you find some you like and add them to your list. Choose these carefully because only three stops are allowed during a routine, including balances performed while in a handstand, split, or scale.
- Experiment with *port de bra* movements, which must be performed while the trunk or the feet are in motion.

Once you have compiled your list, you can begin thinking about required acrobatic passes and dance combinations. Based on your list, decide what each acrobatic pass will be, making sure that the combination you choose includes at least two elements (one of which should be a salto). Next, look at the dance steps you have included in your list. Decide on a sequence that combines two or more elements and note these. Be sure that you have referred to your FIG Code of Points and noted the competitive requirements for beam routines, the value points, and so on.

Theme

Once you have an idea of what the basic core of your routine will be, it is time to think about giving your routine a theme and choosing a style of movement.

Although these elements are not absolutely necessary to a beam routine, they can be very helpful in exploring new movement and adding dimension to the performance.

It is as helpful for the beam as for floor to give the routine a theme that can further develop the composition. Remember that a theme is any identifiable thread that runs consistently throughout the routine, giving it form and continuity. For example, let's say that in experimenting, you find that a movement combination you have come up with seems to be emphasizing circles—circular arm and leg movements such as in figure eights and *rond de jambes*. Or perhaps the movement seems to center on contractions that begin and end in some sort of circular fashion. This, then, is the beginning of a successful theme: Circles and circular movements could be used as a source for developing other movements or combinations that are consistent with this shape. These would then be interspersed throughout the routine.

Let's examine how this circular theme would be incorporated into the routine. Referring back to the list of elements that you intend to use, here are some examples of how a theme composed of circular shapes and movements might be applied:

1. Straddle mount: Slide down into a deep straddle position. Open arms to straight side position, then circle up, over head, down, and back out to side position, punctuating the arm movement with a flick of the wrists for a final pose before moving on.
2. Dance combination: Waltz step forward (RLR). Left arm straight side; right arm sweeps down, forward, up to high fifth position. Repeat waltz step (LRL), executing half-turn as this is done. Left arm remains straight side; right arm sweeps down and out to second position. Step forward on left for preparation and *tour jeté* kicking right. Arms sweep down and up to high fifth, then open to second position.
3. Balance: Perform on one leg, holding opposite leg to back in *attitude* in ring (back leg bent) position. If it is decided that a balance may be needed elsewhere, this position could be kept in motion by simply bending and straightening the support knee after the opposite leg has been placed in the ring position. Some type of complementary movement with the opposite arm might then also be employed.

Keep in mind that a theme can be anything you want it to be. The example of a circular shape is only that—an example. Your theme could just as easily be a feeling or emotion that you use to draw the routine together. You could base your theme on a musical rhythmic pattern. An example of using a rhythmic pattern for theme development might be to try a tango; such a pattern immediately conjures up all kinds of images.

There are an endless number of possibilities that could be used for theme development; the preceding suggestions are just a few examples of how this process works. The important aspect to keep in mind is that using theme development while composing a routine is still another tool to help tap your creative juices when choreographing.

Style

Although the choices of movement are more limited on the balance beam, you can still consider all the basic styles discussed in chapter 6. Choosing a distinct style of movement for your routine will help keep your composition both interesting and creative, as well as enhance the artistic presentation of the gymnast's performance. Once a style choice is made, it should be used consistently with all dance movements and connecting steps throughout the routine. For example, if you find a folk dance style to be appropriate for a particular gymnast, you might have her adopt a coquettish posture, using the hands on hips and shouldering that typify this particular type of movement. Try taking this a step further by experimenting with the rhythmic phrasing of a mazurka, as shown in chapter 4.

Decide on a dance sequence or dance steps and alter them to fit this rhythmic variation. Dance steps that are composed of beats such as those in a *cabriole* have a folk dance flavor and could be used to enhance the routine by further developing this folk dance style.

Perhaps you are working with a gymnast who has a great deal of flair and presentation when she performs. In this case, you might prefer the routine to be more flashy and dramatic. Sharp, staccato, and angular movements that employ hip and shoulder isolation, typical of a jazz style, might be just what you are looking for.

The style choices available are numerous, but again, just as when you are working with a theme, what is important to remember is that simply settling on a choice can make the creative process of developing movement a little easier. Keep in mind that using style as a method for choreographing a beam routine helps add consistency to the movements as well as offers a tool that can be used to develop and explore choreographic ideas.

Creating Interest

As stated earlier, there are certain movement elements that can be used to enhance the flavor of the routine and to add the necessary variety required by FIG regulations. These elements might be considered the icing on the cake, and include the following: rhythmic variation, level changes, directional changes, and movement quality and contrast. Any movement can be altered through one of these movement elements by keeping the movement basically the same, yet changing details in order can be a fairly uncomplicated way to add interest and variety.

Rhythmic Variation

It is understood that FIG requirements state a deduction for monotony in rhythm. What is referred to here as "rhythmic variation" is a mixing of rhythms, phrasing, and tempos throughout the entire routine.

This is very simply a matter of assigning different counts and accents to different movement phrases. You may, for example, decide quite arbitrarily to count a particular phrase in a waltz or mazurka rhythmic structure while giving another movement pass a more syncopated rhythmic structure. Another possibility might be to use a favorite piece of music as a basis for composing the routine, fitting the routine's movements and steps to the rhythmic phrasing and tempo in that particular piece. The variations are both endless and exciting. The point is that by assigning counts to the movement, the speed and rhythm of the performance is altered and monotony prevented.

Level Changes

Obviously, there are some movements in which level changes are inherent, thereby satisfying to some extent that particular requirement. A valdez is one such example. However, to further fulfill this obligation, it is necessary to include movements that also take the gymnast down onto the beam in a sitting, kneeling, or lying position.

In addition to simply having various movements performed at a particular level, one can also take a specific movement and alter the level it is generally performed at. For example, let's refer back to the example for the dance combination given in the preceding section on theme. In this example, two waltz steps were called for, one traveling forward and the second one repeated while making one full rotation. To change the level of this movement, we could perform the first waltz step traveling forward as previously described. The second waltz step could then be taken with the first step traveling forward; the second step executing a half-turn to face back as it is taken; and the third step completing another half-turn to face the original direction, but reaching forward with the step to drop down on the opposite knee as it is completed.

Directional Changes

In addition to level changes, directional changes must also be placed in the routine. These must come at various places on the beam, rather than simply at either end. This is so that the gymnast can avoid monotonously working back and forth from one end to the other.

There are several ways in which this can be accomplished. For example, a movement phrase may begin at one end of the beam, travel to the middle, change to work backward toward the origin of the phrase, then proceed once again on its "forward" path. Another possibility is for the gymnast to travel to the midpoint of the beam, execute a half-turn, and continue traveling backward in the original direction. There are many other possibilities for successfully incorporating directional changes into the beam routine.

Movement Quality and Contrast

Movements showing contrast as well as those using a variety of qualities (sustained, percussive, swinging, and so forth) help make a routine more exciting and interesting to watch. It is particularly important to give serious consideration to both of these elements in a balance beam routine, where movement possibilities are somewhat limited. One of the most unique problems in creating movement on the balance beam is in selecting image-provoking possibilities that can be translated into movement, for example, contrast movements executed from "high to low," using either a sustained or swinging quality, then a percussive quality.

Achieving Dynamic Presentation

More and more gymnasts are being asked to move beyond mere athletic prowess and incorporate artistry into their beam presentations. But what exactly does that mean for the gymnast, and how can she achieve the desired results? What is it that allows a gymnast to transcend a mediocre performance? How can she improve her presentation and achieve a high-quality performance? While there certainly are gymnasts who might be considered "natural" performers, there are some elements of performance that can be identified to help all gymnasts develop a sense of artistry in presentation.

Technique and Control

Obviously, the first step to achieving a quality performance is in the honing of technical skills and the development of control. A solid foundation is required not only in basic tumbling skills but in elementary dance skills as well. Without adequate preparation and training, a gymnast can hardly hope to achieve a level of presentation that could be considered of performance quality.

Confidence

Confidence is another essential ingredient in a gymnast's presentation. Confidence is knowing that when one begins a scale, for example, it will be finished successfully. The gymnast must always have complete faith in her abilities and acquired skills.

Often a gymnast possesses the necessary technical prowess to successfully complete a particular skill, but falls apart once she gets into competition. The execution of a skill is a very black-and-white issue, with no room for luck. If the gymnast has the strength, knowledge, technical skills, and understanding to successfully complete the skill, she can do so. If she doesn't, she can't. The gymnast must understand that, having mastered technique, it is the fundamental belief in her own abilities that makes the difference. Once she begins to doubt her abilities, to lack the confidence to complete a move, she adds the element of chance to the execution of a particular skill. At that point, the successful completion of a skill becomes entirely a matter of luck.

The gymnast who has acquired both strength and technique has the *potential* for successful execution of any skill, but if self-doubt and lack of confidence interfere with a committed execution, she risks the chance of failure. A movement that is performed with hesitation can counteract all other positive components relative to the total picture of that particular movement or skill.

Amplitude

Amplitude in a routine means performing movements with aplomb, finesse, and style. Once the gymnast

has developed the necessary technique and control required to successfully execute the difficult movements in her routine, she must begin to perform those skills with amplitude at every practice.

When the gymnast is not committed to fully completing each part of every movement, we see a very monotonous performance that lacks amplitude. The gymnast must always take every movement to its fullest extension, its highest point, and its deepest level—to "fill the space" with her movements and to make her movements as expressive as possible. To do anything less than this is simply to "mark" her routine, or go through the motions. This makes for a very dull, uninspired, and boring performance.

Amplitude must be practiced. It is every bit as difficult to develop this quality as it is to develop the technical skills and prowess that are mandatory requirements. The gymnast must place as much emphasis on this area as she does on all others.

Focus

When we speak of *focus* with regard to performance, we are referring quite literally to the focus of the eyes during the execution of any movement, as opposed to mental focus to achieve concentration. The use of focus is another essential ingredient in achieving a quality performance. For example, when the gymnast directs her eyes exclusively to the end of the beam regardless of where the complementary focus *should* be for a particular movement, she invariably interferes with the correct line, or look, of that movement.

A perfect example of improper focus can be seen in the execution of a forward body wave. A gymnast who lacks confidence in her presentation often begins the forward contraction while staring diagonally forward at a point on the beam approximately 2 or 3 feet in front of herself. Focusing in such a fashion interferes with the line of the contraction at the beginning of the wave by distorting the vertebrae at the neck. Then, as the movement continues its succession through the spine from the pelvis to the upper back, this gymnast allows her head to tilt backward only far enough so that her eyes remain in visual contact with the beam; this she accomplishes by peering down her nose. Finally, because the neck and head are not completely released at the end of the wave, the movement is not finished with the necessary complete and sustained upper back arch. With this focus and head placement, the entire movement somewhat resembles that of a turtle peeking out of its shell instead of a gymnast performing a body wave.

When the wave is performed correctly, the initial forward contraction should be accented, that is, taken suddenly. Because the contraction is a rounded movement performed with a substantial bend of the knees, the gymnast should be seen to lower herself somewhat toward the beam with a complete curve in the spine from the pelvis to the neck. The second part of the wave is a controlled, smooth transition beginning with a forward contraction, extending through a succession in the spine, and resulting in a back arch position—all of which is initiated by a controlled straightening of the knees. The entire transition is smooth and flowing. Finally, there is a high lifting in the torso, which can be seen to follow the straightening of the legs and the diagonally upward lift of the arms. This lift gives the movement a feeling of suspension, and the final stretch of the spine adds punctuation to the finishing position.

So, within this one body wave, we should have (a) rhythm (the sharp accented beginning, followed by a brief pause or breath, before beginning the smooth succession of the spine); and (b) level changes (a high position when the legs are straight and a low position when the knees are bent).

We can also consider focus in relationship to amplitude. Many a gymnast seems to become hypnotized by the 4-inch-wide apparatus that she is standing on. It is almost as though the gymnast were locked in a room with some sort of attack monster from which she mustn't take her eyes. There she is, going through the motions of performing a particular chore while never letting the monster out of her sight. How well can that chore possibly be completed?

Although this may seem a dramatic analogy, the point of the relation of focus to amplitude is well taken. If the gymnast is concentrating exclusively on the fact that she is standing on a 4-inch-wide apparatus, then the execution of simple arm movements may become gestures that are thrown away instead of becoming high points or accents that accompany the movement. The gymnast must learn to give the same amount of attention to detail to completing all connecting movements and dance steps as she generally gives to execution of acrobatic and tumbling skills. Obviously, a gymnast is fully aware of the dangers involved in not totally focusing on a back tuck, for example. She would no sooner begin the skill without being completely committed to it than she would move on out of it to something else before she had fully secured the landing. Why then is the same consideration not given to the performance of dance steps and connecting steps? The gymnast not committed to fully completing each part of every movement gives a very monotonous performance that lacks amplitude.

Summary

Very simply speaking, we can look at the composition of a beam routine like this:

1. Structure: *What am I going to do?*

Structure can be defined as the compositional nuts and bolts of the routine, the basic core elements that the routine will be built around. In answer to the question "What am I going to do?" one might say, "I'm going to stand up, I'm going to move across the beam, and I'm going to turn around."

2. Theme and style: *Will my movement have an identifiable thread, and what will it look like?*

"Yes, all movements are going to be lyrical, and I'm going to move like a butterfly."

3. Movement methods: *What things will happen along the way?*

"I'll get excited and show rhythmic variation. I'll change my mind and show directional changes. I'll become absorbed in the beauty and color of my wings and show movement quality and contrast."

As for performance, in a broad sense this can be thought of as control and dynamic presentation. It is unlikely that a performer will display dynamic presentation without also demonstrating correct technique. It is equally unlikely that a skilled technician will score high without dynamic presentation. In other words, a gymnast who lacks adequate technique will give a poorly executed performance, and a gymnast who lacks dynamic presentation will give a boring performance.

Simply stated, then, a controlled performance is the result of a solid foundation in basic technical beam skills, whereas dynamic presentation is synonymous with good amplitude, performing movements with aplomb, finesse, and style. Exploring what dance has to offer the gymnast as well as developing the personal artistry of the individual gymnast will go a long way in helping her achieve a quality performance. Use the following Choreography Checklist for Beam to help you get started.

Choreography Checklist for Beam

Directions: There are three parts to this checklist: content, dance elements, and general execution. As in the previous checklist, individual items are listed under each section with a corresponding blank space. As each particular requirement is fulfilled place a check mark (✔) in the space. If an item is not an element you are going to use in the routine, indicate that with an X.

I. Content

In the FIG Code of Points, the term *gymnastic* refers to dance elements, and the term *acrobatic* refers to all tumbling elements.

When the routine is completed, all of the following items should be checked off.

Time 1:10 to 1:30

One acrobatic series, with minimum of 2 elements (1 of which must have flight) _____

At least 1 mixed series (one acro, one gymnastic) of 2 or several elements _____

Balances (no more than 2) _____

Locomotor movements _____

Mount with value _____

Dismount (minimum B value) _____

Minimum level A contained in each pass _____

No more than 2 beam passes in succession without difficulty level of minimum B _____

Distribution of difficulty throughout routine _____

One element/connection close to the beam (sitting, lying) _____

Level changes (excessive sitting or lying position avoided) _____

Direction changes (avoid working exclusively back and forth from one end of the beam to the other) _____

Elements performed in forward, backward, and sideways movements _____

Elements performed in side, cross, and oblique positions to apparatus _____

Movements that show contrast _____

II. Dance (Gymnastic) Elements

Review dance steps and consider ways they can be combined or used to fulfill the following categories.

At least 1 gymnastic series with 2 or more dance elements ⎫ may also be _____
Leaps, jumps, and/or hops (at least 1 with great amplitude) ⎬ component of _____
Turns (at least one 360-degree turn) ⎭ gym/mixed series _____

Connecting dance steps and running combinations _____

Body waves _____

III. General Execution

Fill in this section once the gymnast learns the routine completely. Use this guide to help polish the routine.

Amplitude _____

Rhythmic changes _____

Use of head and facial expressions _____

Avoid focusing directly on end of apparatus exclusively _____

Use of high *relevé* _____

Complete and varied use of upper torso, head, shoulders, and so on _____

Expressive use of carriage of upper torso _____

PART III
Choreography: Putting It All Together

As you begin to choreograph, remember that understanding the principles of classical ballet is the basis of integrating dance technique with the movements suitable for both competitive floor and beam routines. Body placement, balance, line, extension, carriage of the upper torso, and articulation of the feet are all necessary in the execution of any dance style, but the developmental skills traditionally required to perform these principles are rooted in basic ballet technique.

Because ballet technique and its vocabulary are standardized, written choreography describing particular movement phrases does not require a great amount of wordy explanation. Generally speaking, listing the appropriate steps adequately conveys the desired intent. Unfortunately, true classical ballet steps and their corresponding arm placements are not always appropriate for a gymnast's floor or beam routine. In fact, although called on to use many of ballet's standard steps and certainly much of ballet's techniques, the gymnast will rarely put these into any traditional balletic form.

More often, when putting together the dance elements of the routine, the gymnast will need to draw upon other dance disciplines—modern, jazz, and folk—for choreographic inspiration. These dance disciplines, unlike classical ballet, do not have standardized vocabularies. Furthermore, they reflect distinctively different styles that vary dramatically from one to the other. This is particularly evident in the carriage and placement of the arms and the torso.

The lack of a universally standardized dance vocabulary allows for a great deal of style variation even within each of these disciplines, complicating matters still further. Among the three forms, folk has the least amount of variation and jazz the most. Defining a set vocabulary or technique for jazz dancing is complicated not only by the influence of so many

© Dave Black

prominent jazz artists but also by the many movement variations that are possible within the broad technique category known as "jazz dance." Lastly, the movements and steps of modern dance are not founded on any single technique or style; there are several distinctive, accepted styles that have been developed over the years by pioneers in the field. To further complicate matters, modern dance and jazz dance styles often cross lines, making it even more difficult to categorize their movements.

However, the gymnast does not need to be concerned with a strict interpretation of any individual dance discipline. What the gymnast must recognize instead is that the body is a tool for performing movement and that he or she is capable of acquiring creative skills and expressive abilities by becoming familiar with the various dance disciplines. This can only enhance performance and lead to new areas of artistic expression.

The remainder of this book will show how all elements discussed previously can be used in formulating particular movement phrases. Chapter 8 offers prechoreographed movement phrases for floor exercise routines. Then, you will explore methods for composing your own movement phrases for floor (chapter 9) and beam (chapter 10).

CHAPTER 8

Sample Movement Phrases for Floor

This chapter offers examples of prechoreographed movement phrases appropriate for floor routines. These phrases are designed to show how various dance steps, movements, and styles might be combined in a routine. All examples are short, 8 to 16 count phrases. They can be used as given and inserted into a routine, or used as starting bases to be expanded on by your repeating or reversing any portion of the given phrase. Another way of expanding an example would be to add additional movements or steps of your choice to the phrase. For example, if the sample phrase contains one *tour jeté*, you might add a second *tour jeté* or insert a side leap before the *tour jeté*. Another possibility would be to follow the given *tour jeté* with a *tour jeté* and a half-turn.

Keep in mind that the choreographic ideas set down in this text are not cast in concrete and that the tempo and rhythm pattern of any of these examples may be altered to fit the needs of the individual routine. Indeed, it is hoped that you will ultimately find these phrases a means for further developing your own movement understanding and creativity.

Any of the following movement phrases might be used to enhance the choreographic elements of a gymnastic floor routine. These phrases are categorized as classical (ballet), jazz, and folk. Samples of a fourth type of dance, contemporary, are also given in this chapter. This category includes movement sequences that are not of any distinctive style and therefore will fit well with a wide variety of music not representative of any strictly defined musical category.

In each example, the movement style is first identified. Then the time signature is stated, indicating how the phrase should be counted. Finally, the tempo is given to further aid in the understanding and interpretation of the movement phrase.

You may also use this section as a guide for finding appropriate movement for a specific type of music. If, for example, a routine requires movement ideas for music of a folk dance nature, simply choose a phrase that is identified as "Folk Movement Style."

Remember that there is always a certain amount of flexibility with regard to matching music and movement. A classical piece of music may in some instances be performed not only with balletic movements but quite possibly with modern or dramatic movements as well. Although a funky, jazzy musical selection may require jazz movements, contemporary music might be performed successfully with ballet, jazz, or modern movements, depending on its tempo and rhythm. In fact, it is probably safe to say that the only movement limiting musical choice would be folk, which would be best accompanied by folk style music.

Classical Movement Style Examples

Example 8.1

Classical Movement Style
3/4 Time Signature
Moderate Tempo

Movement Phrase

1. Step forward with left and *assemblé* with right. At end of *assemblé*, left arm straight forward, right arm straight side.

Count 1 2

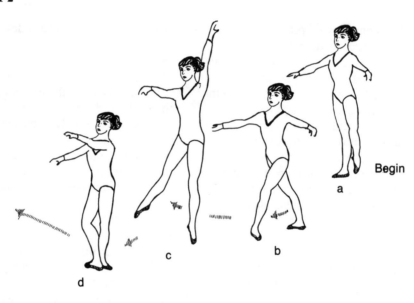

Sissonne forward to open position onto the right leg in *plié*, with the left leg in *arabesque*. Notice that the landing from *assemblé* is the preparation for the *sissonne*. There should be a smooth transition, with no stop, between these two movements.

Count 3

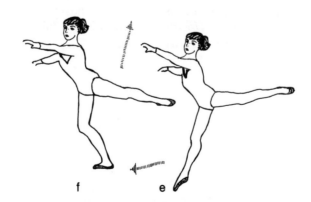

2. Step under with the left leg. *Pas de bourrée* turn so that you face the direction you just came from: Step under with the left foot in *plié*, forward with the right foot on a straight leg and *relevé*, 1/2-turn to the left as you step forward on the left leg into *plié*. Left arm opens to second position as you *pas de bourrée* turn to the left. This is simply a three-step turn with one rotation. The head focuses to the left immediately as you begin the turn.

Count 1 2 3

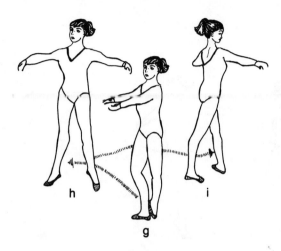

3. *Chassé* forward (LRL). Brush right forward for *tour jeté*. Arms open to second position for *chassé*, lift to high fifth position on *tour jeté*, open to second as you land.

Count 1 2 3

4. Quarter-turn to left following *tour jeté*. Immediately bring the left foot to *coupé* position back. Then *développé* the left leg to side above 90 degrees as you straighten the right leg and *relevé*. Note that the right arm remains in second as you 1/4-turn to bring leg into *coupé* position. Left arm lowers, then lifts through first position and up to high fifth as you *développé* the leg. There is also a noticeable bend in the knees and a downward focus just prior to the side extension, then the accent is up and out as the leg extends strongly to the side.

Count 1 2 3

q   r   s

Sequence Summary

Begin

Example 8.2

Classical Movement Style
4/4 Time Signature
Brisk Tempo

Movement Phrase

1. Slide right leg forward to lunge position to prepare for *attitude* turn to the left on the right leg (left leg *attitude* front). Arms in fourth position middle with left arm forward on preparation for turn.

    As turn is taken, left arm straightens and moves to diagonal up-back position as the right arm straightens and moves to middle front position. Torso is twisted to the left so that right arm is reaching toward the raised foot. Focus eyes out over right hand as turn is taken.

Count 1 2 3

2. Slide left leg to left in *plié*. Arms remain in the same position on the step to the left.

Count 4

Strongly *relevé* and straighten left leg as you lift right leg to *arabesque* position. Forward arm (right) lifts higher to the front on the *arabesque*.

Count 1 2

f

3. *Plié* support (left) leg and straighten as you *relevé* to turn to right, pressing right leg back into *attitude* and then into turned-out *passé* as you continue rotation. As you *plié* to prepare for the outside turn, bring the right arm across the torso to first position. Forcefully open the right arm to second position then immediately up to high fifth as you begin the turn.

Count 3 4

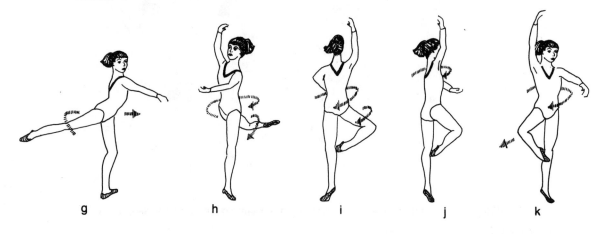

g   h   i   j   k

4. Extend right leg forward to lunge position (preparation for left leg high kick). Lower the right arm from high fifth position to first position as you step onto the right leg.

Count 1 2

l

Execute one full turn to the right with the left leg extended to second position and straightened. Right leg is straight and in *relevé*. Forcefully open the arms to second position as you turn.

Count 3 4

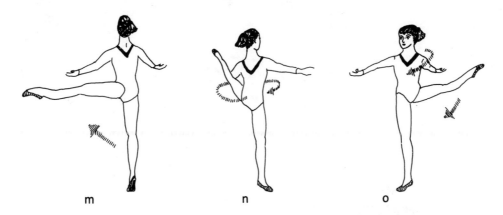

m   n   o

5. Step down onto the left foot across right foot. Perform 1/2-turn to the right, picking up the right leg. Immediately cross right leg back and down to kneeling position. Arms lower beside torso as you step onto the left foot. They lift in a crossed position in front of chest and overhead as the turn is taken, then continue back, down, and out to diagonal back position.

Count 1 2 3 4

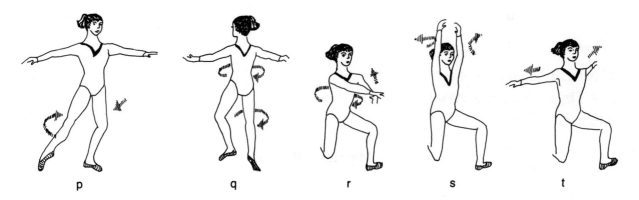

p   q   r   s   t

Sequence Summary

Begin

Example 8.3

Classical Movement Style
3/4 Time Signature (Waltz)
Moderate Tempo

Movement Phrase

1. *Balancé* to the left (step left to the side, cross right behind left and step on right, then step in place with left). Arms move to middle fourth position with the right arm forward.

Count 1 2 3

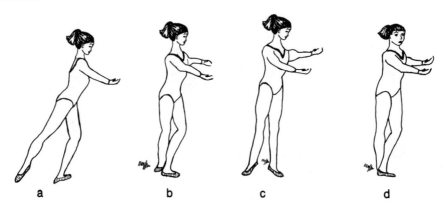

a   b   c   d

2. *Châiné* turn to the right (step on right, then left). Open arms to second as you begin the *chaîné* turn. Close them into first as you take the second step of the turn.

Count 1 2

g   f   e

Soutenu turn to the right (spring from left onto the right, immediately crossing the left over the right, then unwinding as you turn to the right). Arms open again to second position as you begin the *soutenu*. Close them to first. As you rotate, immediately lift them to high fifth as you finish the *soutenu*.

Count -and 3

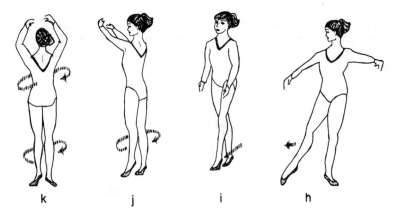

k   j   i   h

3. As you complete the *soutenu*, quickly pick up the right leg as high as possible to the front. Immediately carry it to the side still higher for a *grand rond de jambe*. Finish by lowering the right leg to the back and kneeling. Leave the arms in high fifth as you lift the left leg into *rond de jambe* and kneel onto the right knee.

Count 1 2 3

l   m   n

4. Hold the kneeling position as you perform *port de bras* [not shown]. Sweep the arms into a large circle while keeping them overhead, so that they move forward, side right, back, and side left. Finish in middle fourth position with the right arm front. As you do this, allow the torso to move with the arms.

Count 1 2 3

5. As you rise out of kneeling position, stand on left leg and double *pirouette* on it, turning to the right. Arms cross over head on *pirouette*.

Count 1 2 3

o   p

6. Step to the side with the right leg onto a bent knee. Immediately bring the left leg into *coupé* position back (knee turned out). Open arms to second as step to side with right leg is taken. Lower the left arm to low fifth position as you bring the left leg to *coupé*.

Count 1

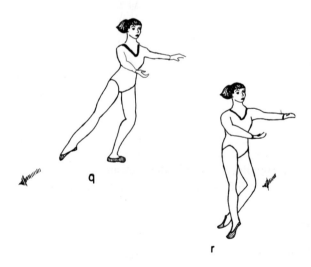

q

r

Strongly *développé* the left leg to the side above 90 degrees. As you do this, straighten the right leg and raise onto the ball of the foot. Lift the left arm through first position to high fifth position as you *développé* the left leg to the side. Right arm remains in second throughout.

Count 2 3

s   t

7. Lower the left leg. Transfer the weight onto a bent left leg as you lift the right leg into *arabesque*. Open the left arm to diagonal back and simultaneously lower the right arm down to your side. Raise it up to front middle as the *arabesque* is taken.

Count 1 2 3

u

Sequence Summary

Begin

Folk Movement Style Examples

Example 8.4

Folk Movement Style
3/4 Time Signature
Moderate Tempo

Movement Phrase

1. Perform *piqué* turn on right (turn to the right on the right leg, picking up the left leg in turned-out *passé*). Step down on left and continue turning on left for outside *piqué* turn (turn to the right on the left leg, picking up the right leg in turned-out *passé*). Open arms to second as you begin the *piqué* turn to the right.

Count 1 2

Soutenu turn to the right (spring from left leg in *plié* onto the right, immediately crossing the left over the right, then unwinding as you turn to the right). The arms remain in second position as you begin the *soutenu*. Close the arms to first and then immediately lift them to high fifth as you finish the *soutenu*.

Count -and 3

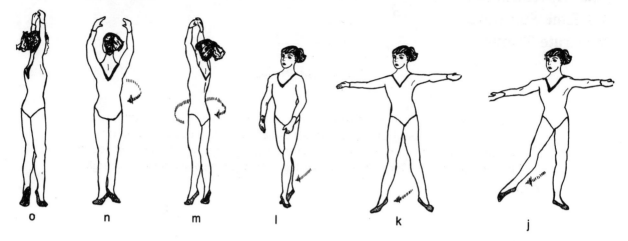

2. As you complete the *soutenu*, quickly pick up the right leg as high as possible to the front. Immediately carry it still higher to the side for a *grand rond de jambe*. Finish by lowering the right leg to the back and kneeling. Leave the left arm in high fifth moving the right arm to the hip as you lift the right leg into *rond de jambe*. Bring arms to your hips as you kneel, elbows pressed forward.

Count 1 2

Quickly slap left knee twice with right hand. Extend the left leg through a bent position and to the side. Straighten the knee as the flexed heel touches the floor. Flick hand at wrist for emphasis as you lift right arm to high fifth position on Count 3.

Count -and-a 3

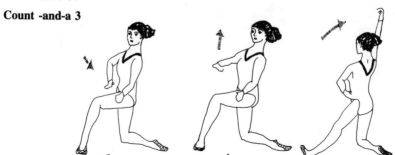

3. Return the left foot to its original support position for the kneel position. Stand on left leg and double *pirouette* on it, turning to the right as you rise out of kneeling position. As you turn, left arm remains on the hip, and right arm sweeps down and out to second and up to high fifth.

Count 1 2 3

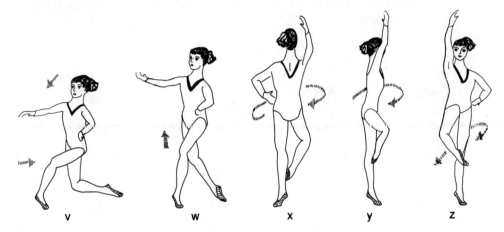

v   w   x   y   z

4. Step to the side with the right leg onto a bent knee. Immediately bring the left leg into *coupé* position back (knee turned out) as you take a small hop in place on the right foot. Left arm remains on hip, right arm opens to second position with palm up.

Count 1 2

bb   aa

Strongly *développé* the left leg above 90 degrees to the side. As you do this, straighten the right leg and raise onto the ball of the foot.

Count 3

cc

5. Lower the left leg and step to the side. Pivot to the right 1/4 so that you can step back with the right. Then cross the left foot over the right so that the top of the foot is resting on the floor (foot pointed) and the left knee is turned out. As you step back with the right leg, strongly sweep right arm forward to first, down beside right leg, and back to circle up overhead to high fifth, again flicking the wrist for emphasis. The arm arrives in high fifth as the left leg crosses the right for pose.

Count 1 2 3

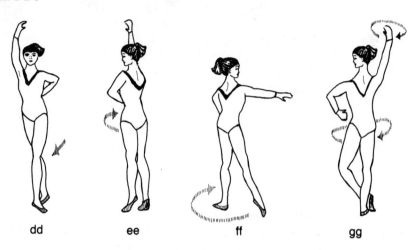

dd   ee   ff   gg

Sequence Summary

Begin

Example 8.5

Folk Movement Style
3/4 Time Signature
Moderate Tempo

Movement Phrase

1. Step right, *coupé* back with left foot, and hop. Move arms to middle fourth position with left arm forward on step-hop to the right.

Count 1 2 3

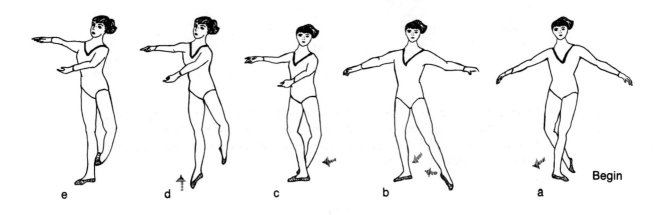

e   d   c   b   a   Begin

Repeat to the left with opposite feet. Move arms to middle fourth position with right arm forward on step-hop to the left.

Count 1 2 3

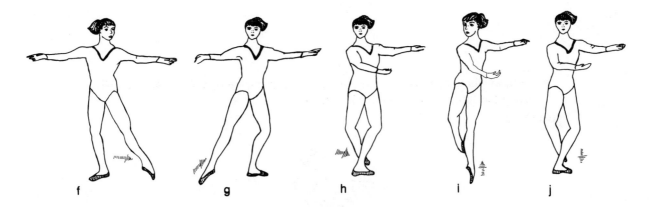

f   g   h   i   j

2. Step right and tuck jump turn one full rotation by tucking left leg, then right leg, into tuck position. Landing is also on left, then right, foot. On tuck jump, right arm moves to hip and left arm lassos overhead.

Count 1 2 3

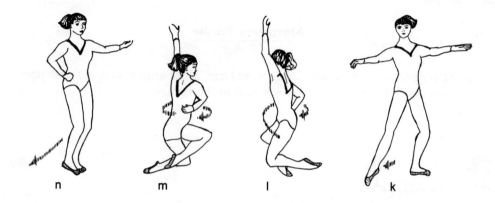

n   m   l   k

3. On landing, take a large step to the side with the right leg. Bend the right knee as you extend the left leg to second position with a flexed foot, heel on floor. Dip torso toward extended leg. As you dip torso forward with flexed heel, both hands move to hips and elbows press forward.

Count 1 2 3

o

4. Shift weight to right foot and *plié* with a little chug on the right foot as you quickly bring the left foot to *coupé* back position.

Count 1 2

p

Extend the left leg 45 degrees to side. Simultaneously, straighten the right leg and *relevé* with a 1/4-turn to the left.

Count 3

Repeat the chug and the *relevé* with leg extension, turning 1/4 to the left to maintain movement flow.

Count 1 2 3

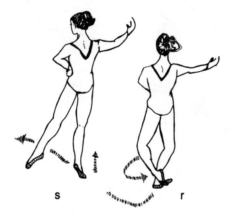

5. Step to side with left leg. Lean forward as you drag right leg behind left to kneel.

Count 1 2 3

Sequence Summary

Begin

Example 8.6

Folk Movement Style
3/4 Time Signature
Moderate Tempo

Movement Phrase

1. Step forward on left. *Ballonné* with right (brush right foot forward and spring off left, immediately bringing right foot to *coupé* front). Hands on hips, left shoulder pressed forward in opposition to right leg on the *coupé*.

Count 1-and 2

Step forward onto right.

Count 3

2. Step back with left and 1/2-turn to face the direction you just came from as you place the right foot to the back in open *coupé à terre*. Strongly press left shoulder back as you step on left and turn to left to *coupé* back.

Count 1 2

g

Hold. Right hand sweeps down then moves through first position to high fifth as you flick the wrist on Count 3.

Count 3

3. Step forward with the right. Skip on right as you brush left foot to the front. Left hand remains on hip. Right hand scoops down, up to first, and open to second position on step-hop. Focus follows movement of hand.

Count 1 2 3

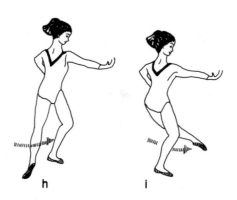

h   i

Repeat skip step with left foot as you brush right foot to the front. Repeat same arm movement with left hand as you step-hop on left.

Count 1 2 3

j

4. Step on right. *Tour jeté* with 1/2-turn, brushing left leg. Sweep arms from low position to high fifth. Open to second as you land from *tour jeté*.

Count 1 2 3

k   l   m   n

5. Immediately take a large step forward with right leg and drag left leg into kneeling position. As you kneel, place left hand on hip and sweep right arm down, back, and up overhead with a wrist flick.

Count 1 2 3

o   p

Sequence Summary

Jazz Movement Style Examples

Example 8.7

Jazz Movement Style
4/4 Time Signature
Moderate Tempo (Movement of lyrical quality)

Movement Phrase

1. Step forward with left. Brush right to side jazz slide. Left arm straight forward, right arm straight side on jazz slide.

Count 1 2

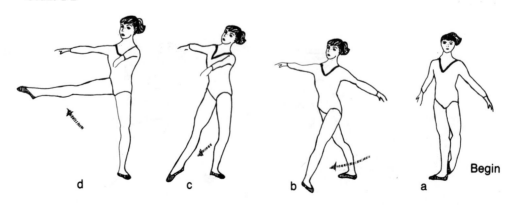

Transfer weight onto right following jazz slide, and step forward with left. Take a small, long, low leap forward onto the right foot, dragging the left foot so that it is stretched behind you and touching the floor. Cross arms in front of chest as you step forward to prepare for leap-drag. Extend left arm to straight middle front and right arm to straight side on leap.

Count 3 4

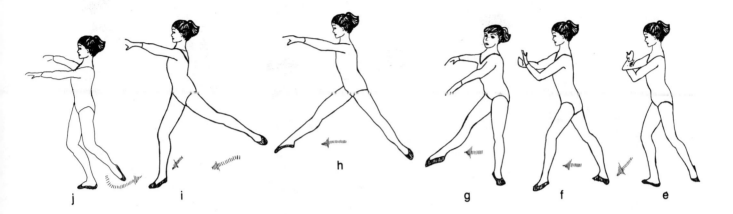

2. *Coupé* back with left. Half-turn to left as you extend left leg front. Meanwhile, right leg remains in *plié* and left hip is up, so torso tilts to the right. As you do this, there is a slight chug (low hop with no weight change) forward on the right foot. As you extend the left leg, left arm moves to straight side position, and right arm remains straight as it cuts down toward side of torso and forward to straight middle front, right hand reaching forward toward left foot.

Count 1 2

3. *Chassé* forward (L R L) and *tour jeté* with right. Arms remain in same position for *chassé*, then cross overhead on *tour jeté*. They lower forward, down, then back to diagonal back position on landing.

Count 3-and 4 5 6

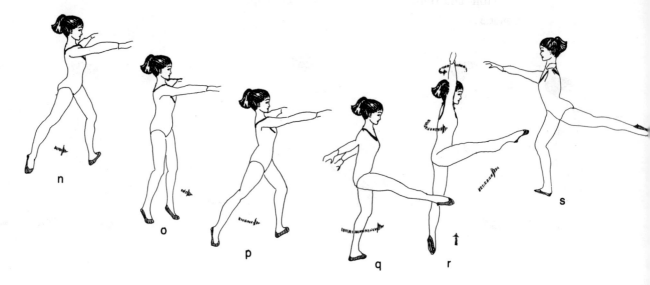

4. Transfer weight onto left from *tour jeté*, and step back and 1/4-turn down onto right knee. Support torso with right hand and extend left leg up to high forward position. Focus out. Left arm goes to straight side position as you step back to kneel. At the same time, the right arm circles back, down, forward, up, and back to reach for floor (windmill).

Count 7 8

Sequence Summary

Begin

Example 8.8

Jazz Movement Style
4/4 Time Signature
Moderate Tempo (Movement of lyrical quality)

Movement Phrase

1. Cross back with the left foot behind the right. Step to parallel second position with right. Step to parallel second with left. Arms at straight side position as you cross back with left foot and open to side with right foot.

Count 1-and 2

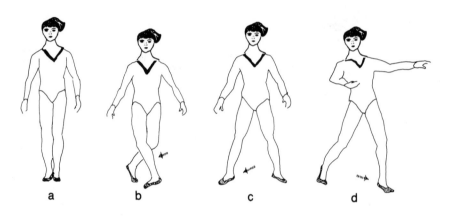

a   b   c   d

2. Outside double *pirouette* on the left leg, picking up the right leg in parallel *passé*. On preparation for turn, place arms in middle fourth position with right in front. Bring both arms to first position in front for *pirouette*.

e   f   g

Immediately place right foot beside left in parallel first position *plié*. Spring up for full turn to the right in the air.

Count 3 4 5 6

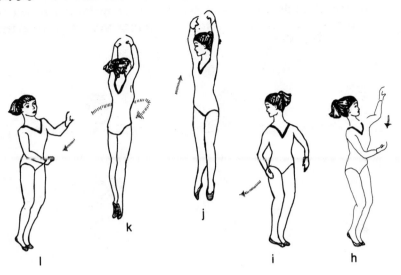

Step on left in place and dig right beside left (parallel first position).

Count -and 7

Step with right to parallel second. At same time, flex the left foot and rest on its heel in second position.

Count -and 8

3. Transfer the weight onto the left foot. Pronate the right knee to pull knee and thigh across and in front of the left leg. Immediately turn out the right leg (knee still bent) and extend it forcefully above 90 degrees to second position. Simultaneously, straighten the left leg and *relevé*. Open arms to straight side position as you pronate knee. Lift arms to straight high fifth position as you extend right leg to high side position.

Count 1 2

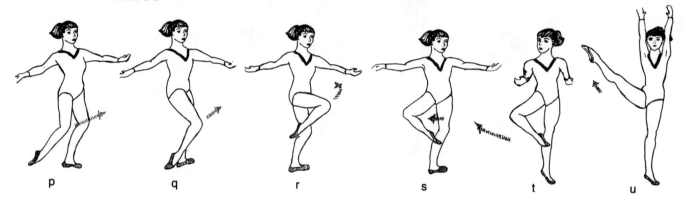

4. Step to the side with the right foot. Immediately cross left leg back to kneeling position. Bring left hand to front middle as you place arms into middle fourth position.

Count 3

5. Knee-spin to the left by bringing the right knee together with the left knee. Lift both arms to high fifth on the knee-spin. Finish one rotation. Sit on hips to prepare for toe-rise.

Count 4 5

6. Toe-rise. As you rise, lower arms down through first position, then back to circle diagonally back and up overhead.

Count 6 7

cc   dd   ee   ff

7. Step forward onto left leg. Lift right leg to *arabesque allongée*, left leg in *plié*. As you step forward with left leg into *arabesque allongée*, the arms press down to circle back alongside the legs and into a straight parallel back position.

Count 8

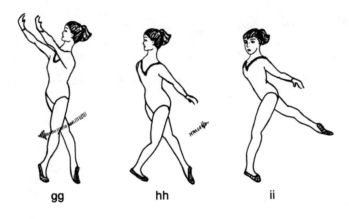

gg   hh   ii

Sequence Summary

Contemporary Movement Style Examples

Example 8.9

Contemporary Movement Style
4/4 Time Signature
Moderate to Slow Tempo

Movement Phrase

1. Step to second position in *plié* with left foot. Right arm is straight side position; left arm goes to box position overhead.

Count 1

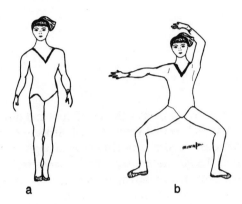

a   b

Straighten legs. Step under torso with left foot. Transfer weight to right foot. Immediately bring left foot to side dig position, both feet in parallel. Left arm moves to low side position; right arm sweeps backward across head and releases down to low side position.

Count -and 2

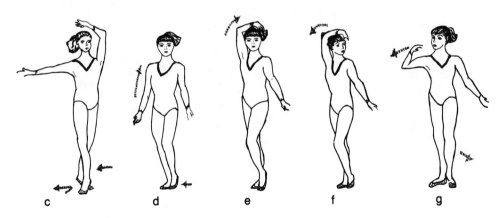

c   d   e   f   g

Open left leg to parallel second position. Turn right knee into pronated position as you step on right. Arms press to straight side position with flexed wrists.

Count -and 3

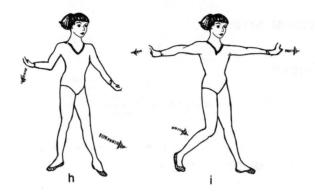

Hold.

Count 4

2. *Pas de bourrée* turn, crossing over with the left foot and turning to the right with right, left. Step to parallel second with left. Lift arms to high parallel fifth position and circle overhead. Parallel arm circle has to begin just slightly before you take the first step of the *pas de bourrée* turn. Arms circle slightly forward, to the right, and to the back before moving to side and lowering into middle fourth position on the third step of the *pas de bourrée*.

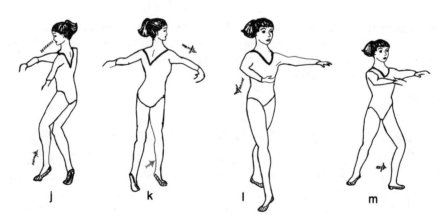

Count 5-and-a 6-and

Outside double turn to the right on left leg. Bring right arm across front of body into fourth position middle as preparation for *pirouette*. Arms go to box position overhead on the *pirouette*.

Count 7 8

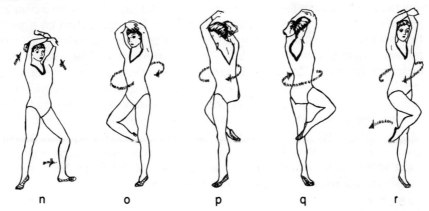

n   o   p   q   r

3. Step down out of turn onto the right foot. Immediately slide left forward to di-agonal position with torso tilting slightly back, then transfer forward into a lunge on the forced arch. As you step diagonally across into the lunge, the arms open in second. Lunge position is with the left knee forward and bent and the left foot raised onto the ball of the foot. There is a very slight contraction in the torso, with the arms in a wide, smooth second position palms up and weight pressed forward over the front leg.

Count 1 2

s   t   u

Transfer weight to front leg (left) as you straighten the back leg and close legs together into fifth position *relevé* with arms in high fifth position.

Count 3   v   w

Open right leg to second *plié* to begin *châiné* turns to the right. After fifth position *relevé*, arms move to middle fourth position with the right arm in front to prepare for *châiné* turn to right. First step of *châiné* turn is taken in second position *plié*. The following steps are all on straight legs and in a high *relevé* position (left, right) except for the last step left, which is again taken on a bent knee so that it serves as a strong preparation for a split leap right. Land on right foot from split leap and immediately tuck left leg under to kneel on left leg. Continue turning to right as you sit on left hip. Open legs through straddle position as you tuck right leg under. Immediately cross left leg over right to stand up on left leg. Arms are in straight side position on turns. Left arm moves to high forward and right arm moves to the side on leap. As you land, the left leg tucks under the right and folds as the torso is lowered smoothly to the ground, with the left hand reaching to the floor for support. As you roll across the hips, the legs open quickly into a wide straddle position, then fold again, with the right leg tucking under so that the left can step across into final pose with left arm back, and right arm down and slightly forward, palm facing out.

Count 4 5 6 7 8

Sequence Summary

Begin

Example 8.10

Contemporary Movement Style
4/4 Time Signature
Brisk Tempo (Dramatic)

Movement Phrase

1. Stand in parallel first position *plié*, arms down at sides. With straight legs, lift to *relevé*. Reach arms up to straight high fifth position.

Count -and 1

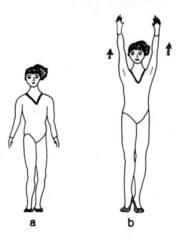

Release suddenly back to parallel *plié*. Bend elbows so that hands come to shoulders on *plié*.

Count -and 2

2. Face left with a sharp, quick step into lunge position, left leg front, right leg back. Shoot arms back up to straight high fifth position on this first lunge.

Count -and 3

Quickly change the direction of your lunge to face the right by turning 1/2 to the right and transferring the weight so that the right foot is front and the left is back. Drop elbows so that hands again come to shoulders. Then press arms with flexed wrists to straight front and side positions as you arrive in this second lunge position. Each of these positions are very clean, punctuated, and separated. Arms and legs must arrive at exactly the same time so that we see four distinct poses: parallel first *relevé*, parallel first *plié*, a lunge with the left foot forward, and a lunge with the right foot forward.

Count -and 4

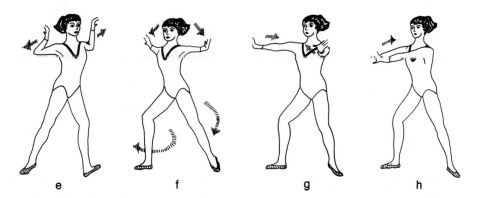

    e   f   g   h

3. Pull weight off lunge and onto back left leg as you turn 3/4 to the right. As you do this, right knee bends and turns out so that the right foot drags across the left foot. On 3/4-turn, leave left arm in second position and pull right elbow back into bow-and-arrow position. This movement contrasts with the first movements of four distinct poses in that all three sections of the turn are smooth and continuous.

Count 5

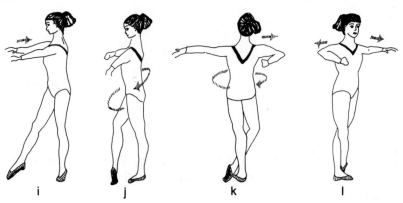

    i   j   k   l

Immediately step to side onto the right foot and execute an inside *rond de jambe* left leg from side to front. Open right arm to second and up to high fifth as left leg is lifted into *rond de jambe*. Left arm remains in second.

Count 6

m   n   o

Step down on the left leg in front of the right. Perform an outside *pirouette*, turning to the right on the left leg, to complete a second rotation. Lift both arms to box position overhead on *pirouette*.

Count 7 8

p   q

4. Immediately step forward into parallel second *relevé* position. Extend both arms to straight high fifth position as you step to parallel second *relevé*.

Count -and 1

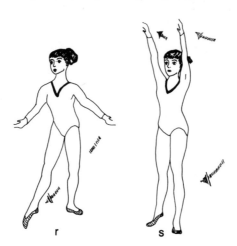

r   s

Lower torso to knees through hinge. Turn palms to face back and lower both arms down and forward in line with thighs as you lower torso into hinge position. As the torso lowers through the hinge position, the knees, shoulders, and hips are seen to be in one straight line at a diagonal to the floor. The knees should be lowered carefully to the floor with control while the torso leans diagonally away.

Count 2

v   u   t

Slide right arm back to elbow support, bend right leg under you, and kick left leg up toward left shoulder. Left palm is placed on floor in front of chest for support as weight is shifted onto right forearm.

Count 3

w   x   y

Lower left leg as you transfer weight forward and stand.

Count 4 5

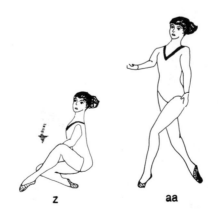

z   aa

5. Step forward on right foot to front walkover. Arms lift, move down to sides, then forward as walkover is taken.

Count 6

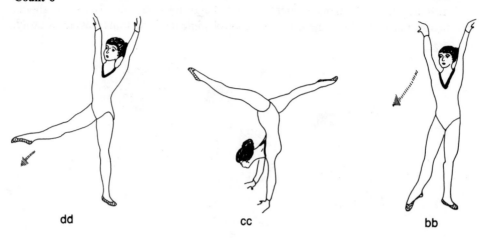

dd   cc   bb

Immediately swing free leg back to *arabesque* position. Arms remain overhead as free leg swings back into *arabesque* position.

Count 7

ee

Drop to chest fall, holding right leg high in split position. Arms circle back, down, and beside thighs, then reach forward into chest fall.

Count 8

gg   ff

Sequence Summary

Begin

Example 8.11

Contemporary, Lyrical Movement Style
4/4 Time Signature
Moderate Tempo (Lyrical)

Movement Phrase

1. Stand in lunge position with left leg forward, arms in straight side position. Hold position. Left arm remains to the side while you lasso right arm over head. Finish with both arms crossed in front of chest for body wave. Move smoothly from the lasso *port de bra* into the body wave so that the two are seen as one continuous movement.

Count 1 2

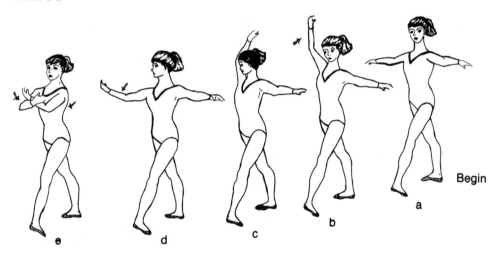

Body wave.

Count 3 4

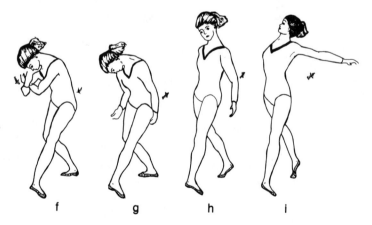

2. Step forward with right [not shown], *tour jeté* with left. Arms optional on *tour jeté*.

Count 5 6

Step forward with right. Kick left leg up into *tour jeté* with 1/2-turn (rotation is to the right), and extend right leg.

Count 7 8

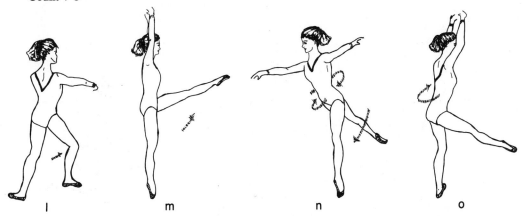

3. Step forward onto right leg, legs in fourth position. Immediately pivot toward back leg and contract torso as you perform sunburst *port de bras*. Sunburst arms reach to right first and end in side left contraction. Sunburst *port de bras* begins with feet flat and knees slightly bent; passes through *relevé* position with legs straight and body stretched; then ends in a contraction with knees bent, arms in, and head down.

Count 1 2

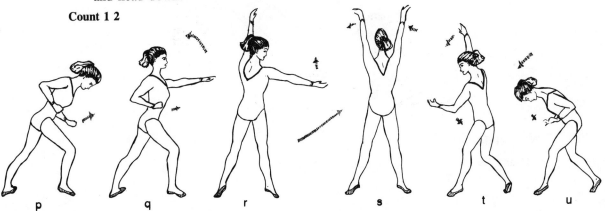

4. Run backward. Then 1/2-turn to face original direction with right, left, right. Arms down on run.

Count 3-and 4

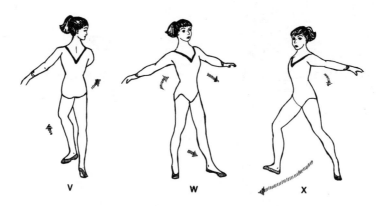

Brush left leg forward into forward jazz slide. Lift arms up-and-back position on jazz slide. Drop immediately to squat position, right knee on floor.

Count -and 5

5. Place right hand on floor behind you. Spring onto feet so that they are in second position, with the weight supported on the right hand and the back arched. Left arm is straight and extended overhead on back arch support.

Count 6

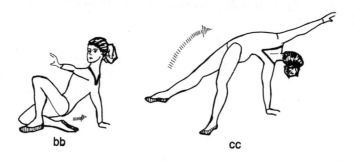

Hold.

Count 7 8

6. Bring left knee into parallel *passé*. Pivot-turn to the right on the right foot; turn one full rotation to sit position with left knee bent and right leg straight. Transfer weight from right hand to left as you pivot on the right leg to sit position.

Count 1-and 2

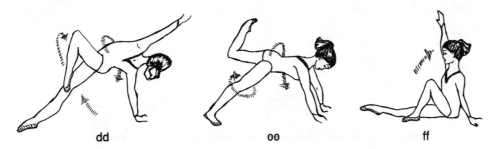

dd   oo   ff

7. Slide down on right side with right arm straight until you are in lying position. As you slide down to lying position, left arm moves forward and overhead, then straight side. Roll onto back and perform double fan kicks with legs (left leg crossing to left and opening right, immediately followed by right leg opening right and crossing left). As you do this, continue rolling to the left until you are on your stomach.

Count 3 4

gg   hh   ii

ll   kk   jj

mm

8. Arms move to push-up position at chest. Lift right leg to *passé* position, then to back *attitude*, as you push up, finally extending the right leg into a standing split position. Keep knee of working leg lifted as you extend into standing split position.

Count 5 6 7 8

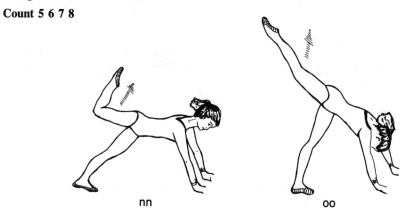

nn   oo

Sequence Summary

Begin

Example 8.12

Contemporary Movement Style
3/4 Time Signature
Brisk Tempo

Movement Phrase

1. Step forward into *arabesque* on the right leg with the left leg lifted. Arms are in diagonal back-and-up position. The back is held very arched and lifted.

Count 1 2 3

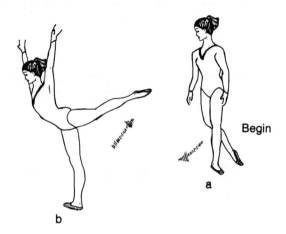

Step forward on the left foot, swinging it quickly from *arabesque* to a forward lunge position. Torso remains lifted as the leg swings through the lunge. Then torso contracts slightly over the front leg, recovers, rolling up through the spine. Note that arms stay stretched overhead to high straight fifth position as you swing leg through to lunge. They circle forward up, down and back to finish once again in the diagonal back-and-up position after you roll through the spine.

Count 1 2 3

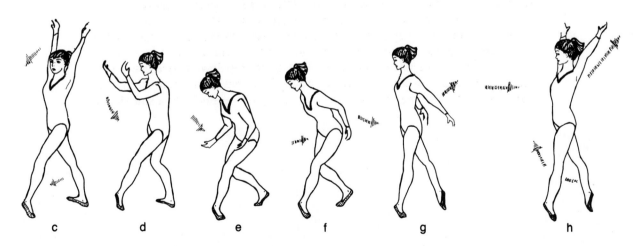

2. *Balancé* to the right (step right, cross back with left, step again on right). Arms go to middle fourth position with the left arm forward.

Count 1 2 3

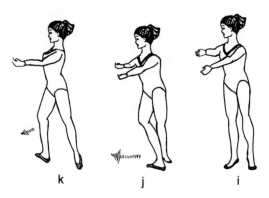

k   j   i

Soutenu turn to the left, stepping on the left and crossing the right over left. Arms move to first position and up to high fifth position on turn.

Count 1 2 3

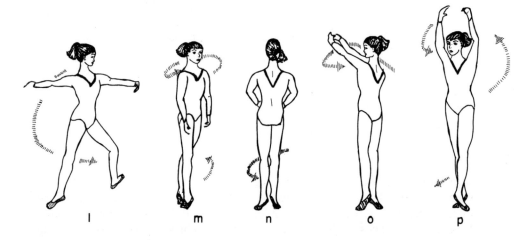

l   m   n   o   p

3. Perform two rotations: The first is on a very straight leg with high *relevé*. Immediately step to the right with the right leg. Turn one full rotation to the right, with the left leg held in second position. After the first rotation, lower left leg to *coupé* position at the side of the right ankle. Draw left up to parallel *passé* as you turn one more time, performing a body wave as you finish this second turn. Arms are straight side on the first turn. Left arm moves in to first and up to high fifth as the second turn is begun. Both arms drop down at sides and swing back, then up and overhead, on body wave. Note that on the second turn the heel lowers and the knee bends slightly so the leg can again lift to a straight leg

with high *relevé* as the body wave is performed. *Balancé* right and *soutenu* left are smooth and connected.

Count 1 2 3

4. Step forward onto left leg and slide right leg back into deep lunge. Arms open to straight side position on lunge. Lunge is taken very deeply so that you transfer smoothly from the lunge to the sit position, then to your side.

Count 1 2 3

5. Sit on left hip and slide left arm out to lie on left side. Roll onto your back. *Rond de jambe* the right leg so that it extends to second position on the floor. Immediately lift the left leg up overhead so that the left leg crosses the torso to touch on the floor to the right. From here, push with the hands so that you are in a split, then a straddle position. Draw the legs together and cross the arms in front of the chest and overhead as you lift into a arch position, taking the arms back to the floor behind you for support.

Count 1 2 3, 1 2 3

6. Lift the left knee to parallel *passé*. High arch in upper back, with focus out and torso supported by arms slightly behind you.

Count 1

Lower the left knee across the right leg and to the floor.

Count 2

kk

Straighten the left leg so that it is parallel to and beside the right [not shown].

Count 3

Repeat the previous movements with the right knee [not shown].

Count 1 2 3

Contract the torso and hug the knees with the arms. Focus is in toward stomach.

Count 1

ll

Strongly extend legs along floor until knees are straight as you sweep arms up and overhead so that torso is stretched and focus is up. Immediately press arms back and down to floor as you arch torso down to lying position on floor.

Count 2-3

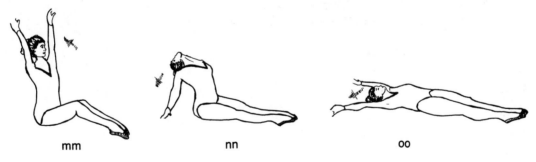

mm   nn   oo

7. *Développé* the left leg to the front and cross it to the floor to the right, left shoulder remains on the floor so that there is a spinal twist from the leg movement. Then roll to the right into a straddle position with the stomach on the floor. Immediately bring legs together and tuck the left toes under as you bring arms to push-up position. Bring right knee to *passé* so that you can press up to a standing split. Try to keep the hips lower than the foot as the right leg extends into the standing split position.

Count 1 2 3

pp

qq

rr

ss

tt

uu

Sequence Summary

Begin

Summary

Exposure to the sample movement phrases described in this chapter will help you as the choreographer see the many possibilities that exist for floor work. These phrases can also be used in classroom practice. Working on phrases and combinations other than the specific dance patterns set in compulsory routines will help the gymnast become familiar with many varied dance movements, contributing to artistic growth and development.

CHAPTER 9

Choreographing Your Own Phrases for Floor

Ultimately, you will want to put together your own movement phrases and routines. Although the choreographic process is largely inspirational, problem-solving is one method that can help you develop your choreographic skills.

This chapter will use problem-solving exercises to help you identify those skills. These exercises are divided into two parts. The first group emphasizes musical time signatures and movement styles such as classical or folk. You will be asked to use these given factors to develop your own movement phrases. The second group of exercises will ask you to use movement qualities, such as percussive or sustained, and spatial awareness in developing movement phrases.

Problem Solving: Musical Time Signatures and Movement Styles

The following section contains four choreographic problems for developing movement phrases. These exercises each emphasize a different musical time sig-

nature and style to guide your creation of a movement phrase. In each problem, you will be given (a) the tempo of the phrase; (b) the type of floor pattern to use in composing the movement phrase; (c) the type of movement phrase to develop, such as a gymnastic-acrobatic combination or a gymnastic combination; and (d) the movement elements to use in the combination.

You are to compose your own combination by following the guidelines stated in the problem. Your combination may be of any length, and it must include all of the elements listed, but the elements do not need to be used in the order given.

Keep in mind that the purpose of this section is to help you develop your creative and choreographic skills. By being given particular elements to use, you can see that although choreographic ideas for some movement phrases may come to you seemingly from out of the blue, you do not need to be totally dependent on divine inspiration for your choreographic phrases. Instead, you can use the examples in this chapter to help you create choreography.

Following each problem, a sample solution will be given to help you see how it can all be put together.

Waltz Combination Problem

Music: Waltz (3/4 time: 1 2 3, 1 2 3, 1 2 3, 1 2 3)
Classical Style
Medium Tempo
Movement Phrase: Gymnastic-Acrobatic Combination

Elements to use

1 leap	2 connecting turns (one full, one 1-1/2)
1 hop	Connecting steps
1 pose	

Possible Movement Phrase Solution

1. Step on right foot. Lift left foot to parallel *passé* as you hop on right. Arms low side right position. Then step forward onto left foot. Arms sweep from low position, through first, to high fifth.

Count 1 2 3

Waltz step traveling forward with right, left, right. Drop arms through first position to low position as you step onto the right foot with a bent knee (count 1). For the next two counts, use a straight leg position in high *relevé* as you step onto the left, then the right foot. Open arms so that left arm is in straight second position and right arm lifts to straight right side, diagonally up (palm facing down).

Count two 2 3

2. Step on left foot. Then prepare on right for inside *pirouette* on right foot. Arms in first position on inside turn (turning to left). Step down on left foot. Immediately perform a 1-1/2 outside turn on the left (turning to left). Arms move to high fifth position on outside turn (on count 3).

Count three 2 3

3. Coming out of the turn, step back on right foot and bring the left foot beside right. Follow with back handspring step out. Immediately swing free leg through to front for *fouetté* to chest fall. Arms lift from low position to high fifth on kick following step out. They remain in fifth position for *fouetté*. Arch upper back to press arms back, then down beside torso to reach forward into chest fall. The raised leg must remain at the established height for the *fouetté* and continue to lift, stretching away from the supporting leg on the chest fall.

Count four 2 3, five 2 3

Hold chest fall.

Counts six 2 3

4. Press arms straight and twist torso toward extended leg to arrive in back arch support on one hand. As you twist torso, weight is supported on right arm. Left arm straight and held overhead. In the back arch position, the right side of the body is favored, the head is back, and the weight is taken primarily on the right leg and arm, the hips pressing up toward the ceiling. The left leg is straight and extended to the side, whereas the support leg is slightly bent.

Count seven 2 3

5. Drop hips to squat position of right leg, left leg extended. Turn to right to stand as you cross left over right and unwind to complete the rotation. Arms held in straight second position.

Count eight 2 3

6. Recover with run, run, switch-leg leap (L, R, brush L). Arms are optional on leap.

Count nine 2 3

7. Land on right. Step forward with left foot. *Grand battement* with right as you raise into the ball of the left foot.

Count ten 2 3

Fall forward into lunge position. Be sure to sustain the *grand battement* just before the lunge so that there is a feeling of suspension before the fall. Arms sweep from low position to high fifth position on *grande battement* and remain there for lunge. Replace right foot with left foot and turn 1/2 to right. Immediately place right in back for fourth position lunge. Focus left on second lunge. Open arms to second position on 1/2-turn. Twist torso to right so that right arm remains second and left arm moves to straight front middle.

Count eleven 2 3

Mazurka Combination Problem

Music: Mazurka (3/4 time: 1-and 2 3, 1-and 2 3, 1-and 2 3, 1 2 rest)
Folk Dance Style
Medium Tempo (Follow standard mazurka rhythm and accents)
Spiral Floor Pattern
Movement Phrase: Gymnastic Combination

Elements to use

2 leaps	Connecting steps of your choice
Movement on floor	1 forward body wave
1 sideways body wave	

Possible Movement Phrase Solution

1. Stand on left foot with right foot in open *coupé* back position, arms down. Step on right and *coupé* back with left, placing left hand on hip, right hand extended to side.

Count 1

Hop on right. Begin figure eight with right arm, crossing in front of torso on hop.

Count 2

Low *développé* front with left as you chug on right. Right arm continues figure eight, crossing in on hop and opening to the side on the chug with *développé*. (Chug is a small, forward-traveling hop in which the foot barely leaves the floor.) Twist torso to the right as you do the step-hop. Twist torso to left as you do the chug.

Count 3

Step on left foot for *chassé* (LRL). Then right together to left in parallel first and *plié*. Open both arms straight side on *chassé*.

Count two-and 2

2. Ring jump with right leg forward, and lift arms overhead.

Count 3

3. Land on right. Bring left foot together with right foot in parallel first position for quick body wave and pose. Cross arms in front of torso in preparation for body wave.

Count three-and 2 3

4. Step forward onto right foot out of body wave. Perform 3/4 inside turn on right leg to finish facing into circle. Immediately step to the left on left foot and perform side body wave.

Count four 2 3

Continuing on path of circle, step back with right foot, pivoting 1/4 to the left on the right foot. High-kick front with left leg, right foot in *relevé*. Right arm lifts to first and up to high fifth, then opens to second on kick; left arm in second throughout.

Count five 2

Change focus to left looking over left shoulder, and immediately pivot 1/2 to the left on the right leg and drop forward into lunge, left leg front. Right arm repeats first to high fifth, then opens to second on pivot, while left arm remains in second.

Count -and 3

5. Run (RL) and kick right up into side leap facing out from circle. Land on right out of leap; cross left over right. Arms are parallel middle front position on leap.

Count six 2-and 3

6. Step to side with right, cross left behind right, and lower yourself onto the left knee. Arms in fourth position middle, left hand front, on kneel.

Count seven 2

Immediately rise out of kneeling position by standing on the right leg. Open left arm to second, and right through first and up to high fifth, as you rise. Also be sure to focus down and right on kneel, then up and left as you rise out of kneeling position. Turn 3/4 on the right leg, turning to the left so that you follow path of circle as you *developpé* the left leg front and *relevé* on the right.

Count 3

7. Step down on left foot, forward on right leg. Immediately cut left under right to replace the right. Then lift the right leg forward into *grand rond de jambe* (right leg lifts front, side, then back). Bring left arm up to join right in high fifth as you cut under for *grand rond de jambe*. Focus up and left as right leg moves to the right in the *grand rond de jambe* (upper body twists left, away from working leg).

Count eight 2 3

8. Tuck right knee behind left to spiral down to knee spin. Drop to left hip, extend torso, and roll to right onto stomach and onto back. Double fan kick with legs, right leg fanning inside, immediately followed by left leg fanning outside. Open arms straight side for spiral to floor. Change focus to right as you begin to sit on hip.

Count nine 2 3

Finish by arching up into pose with right leg bent under, left leg straight and lifted, and torso leaning slightly back to support on hands.

Count ten 2 3

Contemporary-Dramatic Combination Problem

Music: Contemporary (4/4 time: 1 2 3 4, 1 2 3 4, 1 2 3 4, 1 2 3 4)
Contemporary Style
Combine Slow Tempo With Fast Rhythmic Variation
Zigzag Floor Pattern
Movement Phrase: Gymnastic-Acrobatic Combination

Elements to Use:

1 deep lunge   Connecting steps of your choice
1 double turn

Possible Movement Phrase Solution

1. Stand in parallel first with arms down. Step forward into fourth position lunge with right foot forward, crossing arms in front of chest for count 1. Then slice arms to straight side position on count 2.

Count 1 2

Drop left leg back so that you move into a much deeper lunge position. Sharply close arms to middle box position, head lowered between arms. Torso is held erect on first lunge and stretches forward in second lunge as arms close to box position.

Count 3 4

2. Rising out of lunge position, high-kick forward with left leg, then 1/2 turn to right so that kick to front becomes kick to side, right leg straight and *relevé*. Bow-and-arrow arms, right arm back and left extended. Movement of the arms is forceful. The body tilts slightly away from the extended leg. Focus is to left. The extended leg and the arms are both on diagonal lines that should be parallel to each other.

Count 5 6

Following straight-line path, walk forward with left, then right. Arms down at sides on walks.

Count 7 8

3. Step on left. Quarter-turn to left as you sharply extend right leg to side position. Bow-and-arrow arms, now left arm back and right extended.

Count 1 2

Repeat the two walks, again following straight-line path, with right, then left. Arms down at sides on walks.

Count 3 4

4. Double outside turn to the right on right. Arms box position overhead on *pirouette*.

Count 5 6

Sharply extend left leg to low front position, and arms to straight side; *plié* on base (right) leg as the leg flicks to the front at end of turn. This movement begins where the straight-line path becomes a zigzag pattern.

Count 7 8

5. Step to front aerial.

Count 1 2

Repeat aerial.

Count 3

Step forward out of aerial. Lower back leg to deep lunge position. Right arm circles up, back, and forward (this last movement is as though you are throwing something forcefully). At the same time, the left arm moves forward to box position and covers face as head turns away. Slight torso contraction and twist to left on final lunge position.

Count 4

Contemporary-Jazz Combination Problem

Music: Contemporary (2/4 time: 1 2, 1 2, 1 2, 1 2)
                                         >   >   >   >
Jazzy Style
Quick Tempo, Combined With Some Pauses for Rhythmic Variation
Zigzag Floor Pattern
Movement Phrase: Combination Gymnastic-Acrobatic

Elements to Use:

Hops or skips	2 leaps
1 leap-turn combination	1 body wave

Possible Movement Phrase Solution

1. Stand in parallel first position with arms down at sides. Ring jump. Arms in V position overhead. Cross them in front of chest on landing from jump.

Count 1 2

2. Cross left over right as you land. Immediately jazz slide to right. Straight arm fourth position on slide, left arm front. Base leg remains slightly bent on jazz slide. Head focuses to right. Right foot touches floor at end of jazz slide, but no weight is placed on right so you can immediately step back with right again for next movement.

Count -and 1

3. Step back with the right foot as you step forward with the left into parallel fourth position *relevé*. Arms bend so that hands touch shoulders and elbows are lifted to front middle position as you step back with right foot. Focus is down on the step back; focus up on the *relevé*. Both legs straighten as you step into the *relevé* position.

Count -and 2

Hold.

Count 1

4. Travel backward with 1/2-turn to right as you run right, left. Focus over your right shoulder, and sharply extend arms overhead to straight side position.

Count -and-a 2

Cat-leap full turn to right (lift right, then left). Arms high fifth.

Count -and 1

Side leap with right leg leading. Left leg crosses over right on landing. Arms straight front middle on side leap, palms up.

Count -and 2

5. Twist 1/2 to right as you step and open feet into parallel second position (RL). Press arms to straight side position with palms flexed.

Count -and 1

Bring right, then left, together into parallel first position *plié*.

Count -and 2

Repeat twist with 1/2-turn to right, again stepping into second position with right, then left. Repeat press to second position with arms.

Count -and 1

Repeat release of feet to parallel first position *plié*, and cross arms in front of chest.

Count -and 2

6. Step with right to parallel *passé* and hop. On hop, swing arms down and up to left arm straight side, right arm straight overhead. Look toward left hand on the hop.

Count 1

Step left and split-leap with right. On leap, left arm straight middle front, right arm straight side.

Count 2

Land on right and make switch-leg leap with left.

Count -and 1

Bring feet together to parallel position for body wave.

Count 2, 1 2

7. Back handspring, walkout, back salto, straddle jump.

Count (Use number of counts necessary to complete tumbling phrases.)

Problem Solving: Movement Qualities and Spatial Awareness

The following three choreographic problems emphasize movement qualities and spatial variations in developing the movement sequence. Each problem will state (a) movement quality, such as percussive, sustained, or swinging; (b) spatial variations, such as level changes or directional changes; and (c) movement elements to use. You are to compose your own phrase by following the guidelines given. You may use any time signature you like, but compose a phrase that is 4 measures in length. For a 4/4 time signature, for example, this would be 4 measures of 4 counts each, or 16 total counts in the phrase.

Because the emphasis in these problems is on movement quality, you are given only one or two mandatory elements. Fill the other counts with your choice of turns, leaps, connecting steps, forward or backward acrobatic skills, and so on. Each problem will be followed with two possible solutions for your reference. This is so you can see how the same basic movements may be altered to adjust the level of difficulty, the rhythm, or the style of movement.

Problem 1

Swinging Movement Quality
Spatial Variation: Level Change

Elements to use

Leaps

Problem 1, Solution A

Jazzy Style
4/4 Time Signature
Quick Tempo

1. Stand in parallel first position, legs straight and in a high *relevé*, arms straight overhead. (Perform movement on a straight-line path.) Movement begins facing 90 degrees from the straight-line path. Step forward onto a bent left leg and back with right into lunge. Allow body to execute 1/4-turn to the right as this is done. Turn palm to face back. Rotate arms as they press down and then forward to front middle position, with palms up. Note that the step into a lunge position places you facing the direction of the straight-line path.

Count -and 1

Hold.

Count 2

2. Turn to right as you transfer lunge so that the right foot replaces the left and the left steps back. This lunge is a half-turn so that you are now facing the opposite direction but still moving on the straight-line path. Bow-and-arrow arms, right arm back and left arm forward. On the bow-and-arrow movement, there is a substantial twist in the torso, making the left shoulder almost in line with the right knee. The focus is out toward the extended arm.

Count -and 3

3. Pivot 1/4-turn to the left on base left so that the left leg rotates from lunge position to side position and the right leg is raised to 90 degrees. Pull left elbow back so that left hand touches left shoulder. Right arm reaches straight up and overhead. Focus up toward right hand. Extended leg is raised as high as possible,

at least above 90 degrees. There is a feeling of being suspended from above on this movement.

Count 4

4. Cross right over left, and do two *chassés* (LRL, RLR). Step left and *tour jeté* with 1/2-turn at the end. Arms at straight side position for *chassés*. Then lift arms to high fifth. Open arms to second on *tour jeté*.

Count 5-and 6

5. Run, run (LR). Switch-leg leap with left. Arms straight side position.

Count 7-and 8

6. Back walkover. As leg lands, maintain a high split position with second leg. Immediately rotate to back layout arch position. Arms remain overhead for rotation. Then circle forward, down, and back as you execute upper back arch release before recovery to upright position. Leg remains as high as possible out of the back walkover as you rotate and twist the torso to face the extended leg. Be sure to pivot on the ball of the standing leg as you rotate to face the extended leg.

Count 1 2 3

Hold.

Count 4

7. As the arms circle and you perform the upper body arch, raise onto the ball of the base foot, and then fall forward into lunge position. Contract arms sharply into torso.

Count 5

Hold lunge position, and pendulum swing arms two times, beginning with right forward and left back.

Count 6 7 8

Problem 1, Solution B

Folk Style
2/4 Time Signature
Moderate Tempo

1. Begin facing in the direction of the straight-line path. (Perform movement on the straight-line path.) Step on right and hop. Arms swing to fourth position left arm front.

Count -and 1

Step on left and hop. Arms swing to fourth position right arm front. Note that these movements begin traveling forward. Hops are performed with free leg in *coupé* back position. Head focuses to the right, then to the left.

Count -and 2

2. Face sideways and place right foot into parallel second *plié*.

Count 3

Slide to right (L foot replacing R). Finish in parallel second position. Immediately lift left leg to parallel *passé*. Alternate shoulder shrugs on slide, beginning with left up, then right, then left. Slide is taken as the body turns sideways but travels on the straight-line path. Movement finishes with left knee and left shoulder both lifted.

Count -and-a 4

3. Step with 1/4-turn to left onto ball of left foot in dig position. Then immediately transfer weight onto flat left foot, and open right leg forward onto the heel. Arms reach straight overhead. They press down to middle front and open to side with palms flexed so that left arm is front, right arm back. A 1/4-turn puts you once again on straight-line path, but facing opposite direction from which you started.

Count -and 5

4. Half-turn to left as you step onto the right into parallel first position. Immediately bring the left foot together with the right. Contract arms into chest.

Count -and 6

5. Quarter-turn to left, stepping to parallel second position with right, then left. Press arms to straight side with palms flexed up. Continue turning left so that you are again facing sideways on the straight-line path.

Count -and 7

Recover by bringing legs together into parallel first position and *plié*. The recovery into parallel first is a contraction with knees bent and focus down.

Count -and 8

6. Half-turn to right as you perform jump tuck. Quickly extend right leg forward as you land on left. Step forward into front aerial. Arms slide side as leg kicks out. You are now facing the original direction on the straight-line path.

Count 1 2 3

Hecht dive with 1/2-turn. Immediately stand and drop left leg back to fourth position lunge. Wrap arms and torso to right as you step into lunge.

Count 4 5 6

Step into lunge position, forward on left leg and back on right. Press arms out to second as you change legs in lunge. Torso twist to the right. Focus is down and to the right on lunge. Focus changes sharply to left on second lunge.

Count 7 8

Problem 2

Swinging Movement Quality
Spatial Variation: Level Change

Elements to use

2 full turns

Problem 2, Solution A

Contemporary-Dramatic Style
4/4 Time Signature
Slow Tempo

1. Stand in parallel first position *plié* with arms crossed in front of chest and head lowered and torso contracted. (Movement travels in circle pattern.) Body wave.

Twist torso immediately to left and finish in torso contraction. Standard arm accompaniment for body wave, finishing in toward torso on contraction. Complete the body wave so that the focus is up at the height of the movement. Then move sharply into the side contraction position.

Count -and 1

2. Arms remain left with focus as you open right leg to side lunge position for slide to right, finishing in side lunge position with weight on right foot.

Count 2

Again, left replaces right, right opens side as slide to right is repeated, finishing in side lunge position with weight on right foot. Both arms swing to right in figure eight pattern as focus changes on the slides. Follow hands with eyes as arms sweep in side circle.

Count -and 3

Immediately transfer weight over to left and contract torso. Then *plié* in deep second position as you swing body through *grand plié* from left to right as you turn to face the right leg. Lift the body and left leg into *arabesque*, base leg remaining bent. On contraction and *plié*, arms continue movement to left, down, and then right. Finish arms with left middle forward and right diagonal back on *arabesque*.

Count 4 5

Hold.

Count 6

3. *Pas de bourrée* turning left (LRL). Arms fourth position middle, front. Look over left shoulder for *pas de bourrée* turn.

Count 7-and 8

Cat-leap turn continuing to left. Arms move to high fifth. Continue focus over left shoulder for cat-leap turn.

Count -and 1

Land on right and continue turning left. Open both arms side as rotation is finished. Note that the step right, then left, out of leap should complete two rotations (720 degrees).

Count -and 2

4. Step forward on left and drag right foot in back, both knees bent. Perform forward body wave, lifting back leg up to *arabesque* immediately on recovery from arch of body wave. Arms cross in front of torso as in a figure eight. They immediately swing down and back for body wave. Both arms straight and overhead on *arabesque*.

Count 3 4 5 6

5. Step back on left and transfer body into backward lunge. Arms remain overhead as you bend torso down over front leg. Sweep arms back to diagonal up-and-back position as you lift torso.

Count 7 8

Problem 2, Solution B

Jazzy Style
4/4 Time Signature
Quick Tempo

1. Begin facing inward for traveling in a circle pattern. Step into side lunge position with left leg. Lift both arms to side middle left position. Circle down, right, overhead, and back to side middle left. Focus follows arm circle.

Count -and 1 2 3

Transfer weight to right and execute a right turn with left leg in second position (one full turn). Arms open straight side second position on turn. In second position turn, the arms must be extended directly to the sides for a very stretched position. The base leg is straight and in high *relevé*. The lifted leg is also stretched out and away from the body.

Count 4

Pull free leg quickly into parallel *passé* (second full turn). On count 5, parallel *passé* is taken on a bent knee and is used to stop the turn. As the rotation is completed, the body should begin to slow. Then pull firmly into the parallel position, bending the base knee. As turn is completed and knee bends into *passé plié*, place arms in middle fourth position, right arm front.

Count 5

Step down on left across right and slow spiral turn, continuing in same direction. Legs bend as you step down to begin spiral and straighten as you continue the third full turn. Figure eight arms left to right on spiral turn. On count six, of the spiral turn, the legs are crossed and opened (fourth position).

Count 6 7 8

2. *Chassé* (RLR) brush left into *tour jeté*. Arms straight side position on *chassé*.

Count 1-and 2

Tour jeté (brush L, land R). On *tour jeté* lift arms to high fifth and open to second.

Count 3 4

3. Step to side for side body wave to left.

Count 5-and 6

4. Cross right leg over left and pivot one full turn to left. Immediately lift left leg to fan kick, then fall into left leg lunge. Arms straight side on pivot. Lift right arm to high fourth position on fan kick. From the pivot and as the leg lifts into the fan kick, the base leg straightens and rises into *relevé*.

Count 7 8

Problem 3

Percussive or Sustained Movement Quality
Spatial Variation: Circular Movements

Elements to use

Body wave   Leap or turn

Problem 3, Solution A

Waltz Style
3/4 Time Signature
Moderate Tempo

1. Begin standing in parallel first position. Face out away from the figure eight of the upcoming floor pattern. Take a large step to the side with the right foot into *plié*. Lift the left leg to second position. Sweep both arms down and to the right side middle as you take the step into *plié*.

Count -and

With left leg remaining in the air, slowly twist torso to left as right leg moves forward against the torso twist; sustain this. As you twist torso, move arms straight across torso through middle front, to middle fourth position, with right arm front. In the sustained position, the base leg is in *plié* and the extended leg is stretched away from the torso. Focus is in the direction of the raised leg.

Count 1-and 2

Allow movement to pull your weight off balance: Fall off the base leg onto the left foot, crossing it over the right to take the step.

Count 3

Step back with the right foot.

Count and

2. Immediately step onto the left foot, taking a 1/2-turn to the right so that you are facing in toward the figure eight pattern. Simultaneously lift the right leg to second position. Repeat same arms in opposite direction.

Count 1

Repeat slow, sustained torso twist so that leg moves forward as torso twists to right.

Count 2 3

3. Cross right over left as weight is pulled backwards and off balance. Continue moving to left as you step with left, then right. Arms straight side.

Count 1 2 3

4. Step forward on right and drag left through *coupé* back position. As you do this, begin to *développé* the left leg forward, but allow torso to turn 1/4 to the right away from the *developping* leg so that the *développé* is actually facing side. As you do this, allow torso to tilt directly to side and away from the raised leg into a right torso tilt position. Both arms drop down. Then, remaining straight, they cross to right, lift to side middle, and finally lift to straight high fifth position as tilt is taken. Step to *coupé* is taken on a bent leg, which straightens as body turns and leans into side tilt position.

Count 1 2 3

5. *Chassé* (LRL). Arms middle fourth.

Count 1-and 2

6. Step right, then *tour jeté*, kicking left leg forward. Lift arms to high fifth position. Open to second on landing.

Count -and 3

7. Step forward to parallel first position. Swing arms down, forward, and up to straight high fifth position. The step to parallel first in *relevé* is a pose. It is a very stretched, extended position with the focus up.

Count 1

Drop to floor; sit on right hip and slide down to support torso with right elbow as you extend left leg up in air. In the final pose on floor, right leg is bent and on floor, while left leg is stretched to the ceiling.

Count 2 3

Problem 3, Solution B

Contemporary Style
4/4 Time Signature
Quick Tempo

1. Step forward with right leg into lunge position. Immediately kick left leg to high front position. As you do this, the right leg straightens and lifts to *relevé*. Punch left arm forward and right arm back to bow-and-arrow. Accent first and second counts by moving strongly into position.

Count 1 2

2. Take three small runs forward in *plié* (LRL). Arms down on run.

Count 3-and 4

Close right leg behind left, both legs now bent. Spring up into the air for one full jump turn, kicking the right leg forward at end of turn as you land on the left leg in *plié*. Arms move overhead for turn; accent is on jump.

Count 5 6

3. Fall forward onto right in *plié*. Immediately straighten right leg to *relevé* as you lift left to turned-out *passé*. Body is in arc position. Arms sweep down, to side right, and overhead toward left for arc position on *passé*. The hips are pulled forward and slightly off balance from the base leg which is counterbalanced by the shoulders and arms as the arc position is formed.

Count 7 8

4. Travel forward with step left and skip. Arms swing to left.

Count 1-and

Step right and skip. Arms swing to right.

Count 2-and

5. Back up, stepping with left, then crossing right over left.

Count 3-and 4

6. Step back again with left and 1/2-turn to kick right leg into side leap. Arms parallel middle front position with palms up on side leap.

Count -and-a 5 6

Land right, cross left over right on landing, and immediately jump up to ring jump. Arms over head on ring jump.

Count 7 8

Summary

Working with the preceding choreographic problems will help you understand the various aspects involved in the compositional process. As you become more secure with the process, try to use this problem-solving method as a guide for altering or developing your own phrases.

CHAPTER 10

Choreographing Movement Phrases for Beam

Creating interesting visual images with the body is very important on the balance beam. The emphasis on visual pictures is even greater here than on the floor, where the working space of the gymnast is not as restricted. When composing routines we very often depend too heavily on standard steps and poses, while ignoring the potential for creative movements that may fall outside a standard movement repertoire. Improvisation can be one method for exploring this potential. When developing movement appropriate for a routine, improvisation only begins with a certain situation instead of being specific, prescribed movements or steps that are incorporated into a movement sequence beforehand.

Developing Improvisational Movements

Improvisation means to invent or compose. With movement, we can accomplish this in several ways. One method is to use some image or emotion as the thematic or stylistic basis for movement that is completely original, that does not fall into any particular category of standard dance steps, poses, or arm movements. Many standard arm movements or *port de bras* common to jazz dancing probably originated in this way. The sunburst *port de bra* described in chapter 2, within the section ''Arm Movements in Nonclassical Positions,'' is one such example.

Another way of developing improvisational movement is to create a situation that can be described in movement. In this method, both original and standard movements may be combined to interpret the theme or idea involved in the situation. These movements might begin as very literal depictions of the given idea, which are then embellished and expanded to become more appropriate for a routine. Following are examples of situations that you might use as improvisational exercises:

* Splashing in and out of consecutive puddles after a rain
* Responding to a clap of thunder
* A flower opening up its petals to the sun
* An electrical storm with lightning striking
* Waves rushing ashore

For this exercise you may choose one of the examples just given or create a situation of your own.

Once you determine the situation, try to find a movement that describes that situation. Then embellish it a little further so that it can be transferred into a movement phrase on the beam as exemplified in the following problems. When this is accomplished, intersperse acrobatic skills where appropriate. Once the phrase is complete, supply your own counts to add interest and rhythm to the movements.

Improvisation can be a very effective method for exploring potential movements for a balance beam routine. Following are two improvisational situations for you to develop into routines. Possible solutions are given for each example.

Problem 1

1. **Catch a balloon floating by.**
2. **Relate to its roundness.**
3. **Release the balloon into the air.**

Problem 1, Solution A

1. Begin with feet in parallel first position, arms down at sides. *Plié*, *relevé*, and sweep arms upward to high parallel fifth position.
2. Bend knees and contract elbows into ribs, upper torso facing diagonally out to left side as torso contraction is executed to left. Follow with parallel figure eight arms with spinal contraction to right. Finish with torso contraction to left. Figure eight arms will begin downward and to left. To execute the spinal contraction, perform a small upper body wave as arms complete half of figure eight. Repeat body wave to right as arms perform second half of figure eight. Arms travel through finish high fifth position as legs straighten before continuing figure eight to end in left side contraction.
3. Remain in left torso contraction in *plié*, and lift right foot to left knee into parallel *passé*. Then, *relevé* and extend right leg above 90 degrees to front. As this is done, pendulum swing left arm forward, while right arm moves in overhead sweep to straight middle back position.

Ending the Phrase Solution   **A**
Continue moving out of phrase with a • front walkover, • front aerial, or • *chassé* split leap.

Problem 1, Solution B

1. Stand on right leg and point left foot forward. Step-hop on left and lift right to parallel *passé*. Torso slightly contracts as arms sweep down on the step, and up to high fifth position on the hop. Torso extends upward as arms lift to high parallel fifth on the hop.
2. With arms still in parallel high fifth position, extend right foot forward to lunge position. Then drop torso forward over right knee. Allow the body to roll backward through spine to upper back arch position. Arms simultaneously execute parallel full circle front to back.

   Note that the body wave will be seen as one continuous sweep. Arms remain in high fifth until torso is fully extended over right knee. The arms then drop down, then back, and finish in high fifth as the movement progresses successively through the torso to upper back arch position.

   From body wave, recover torso to upright position. Then close back leg to front and straighten right leg to complete a back *soutenu* with 1/2-turn to left, allowing toes to pivot.

3. Transfer weight to right leg. Lift left knee, placing toes to side of right knee into parallel *passé*. Contract torso bringing right elbow to left knee. Bend base knee and in this position begin 1/2-turn on the right leg to the left. As the turn is performed, focus down.

Straighten right leg, rising onto ball of the foot into *relevé* position and *développé* forward with left. As turn is executed, arms will pendulum swing in opposition (right arm front, left back).

```
┌─────────────────────────────────────────────┐
│ Ending the Phrase Solution          B        │
├─────────────────────────────────────────────┤
│ Continue moving out of the phrase with a      │
│  • cartwheel,                                 │
│  • side aerial,                               │
│  • chassé split leap, or                      │
│  • cartwheel to handstand balance.            │
└─────────────────────────────────────────────┘
```

Problem 1, Solution C

1. Facing sideways on beam, stand with weight on left leg and place the ball of the right foot next to the instep of the left foot in dig position. Execute sunburst arm movement left to right, and open right leg to side lunge position using the following suggested timing for the arm movement: Shoot right, then left arm diagonally out to left side, which places torso into a side tilt position (count -and 1). Torso straightens and both arms swing overhead to right (count -and) as *relevé* with feet in second position. Step right to side lunge as right arm contracts into side. Left elbow pulls into ribs and torso twists slightly to right (count 2).
2. Turn right foot out as you extend the left arm middle front, then overhead, and press down to middle back position. Right arm lifts to first position. Body is now facing end of beam with focus out. Take a 1/4-turn to right. Lift left leg to parallel *passé*. Arms perform full parallel circle back down and front, finishing with right hand on knee, head down, and torso contracted.
3. As body lifts out of contraction, right arm leads into reverse windmill. Then, both arms stop and hold in high fifth position as leg extends to backward scale.

```
┌─────────────────────────────────────────────┐
│ Ending the Phrase Solution          C        │
├─────────────────────────────────────────────┤
│ Continue moving out of phrase with a          │
│  • cartwheel back walkover,                   │
│  • cartwheel back handspring, or              │
│  • cartwheel back tuck.                       │
└─────────────────────────────────────────────┘
```

Problem 2

1. Pick up a large beachball.
2. Throw it toward some target from overhead.
3. Move forward to get a better look.
4. React to the throw.

Problem 2, Solution A

1. Standing in parallel position approximately 3 feet from end of beam and facing opposite end, slide left leg back to deep lunge position. Simultaneously circle arms back and overhead as torso descends, allowing back to arch during arm circle. At depth of lunge, sweep arms down toward beam and up to cross in front of chest. Circle both arms down toward the right side of body, back, then up as you lift the chest to stand, recovering from the lunge by straightening the right leg and pointing the left leg to *tendu* back. Allow upper back to arch as you circle arms down and back.

    As you recover to the standing position, the focus is straight forward. The arms are to the right and back, the left arm crossed in front of the body.
2. Allow the palms to flex as you forcefully press hands forward until arms are extended and at middle front position. At the same time, lift left leg straight up to front position while rising on the ball of the base leg. This is a very extended position, with the torso stretched upward against the forward thrust of the arms and the leg.
3. Step forward on left leg and *assemblé* forward with right. Meanwhile, arms press open to straight side position. Immediately jump, tuck, then land on left. Extend right leg forward on landing. Right arm sweeps down, then forward, up and back as torso twists to the right; left arm moves to straight middle front position; while right arm drops to and holds in diagonal down-and-back position.
4. Step forward onto right leg. Left arm moves straight up and overhead on the step; right arm remains in diagonal down-back position allowing torso to twist to the right with focus straight forward. Pivot on right foot so that you face opposite end of beam. Step onto left foot. As step onto left is taken, turn left palm to face back and press left arm down and back. Meanwhile, right arm swings down, then moves forward. Head drops down as hand reaches up over the head; elbow is bent and head is "buried" into arm. Left arm stops in diagonal down-and-back position. In this final pose the weight is on the left leg with a slightly bent knee; right leg is back and also bent, the foot pointed so that top of foot rests on beam. Torso is contracted and twists slightly to the left.

Problem 2, Solution B

1. Starting at end of beam, step forward onto the right foot as you circle the right hand forward middle, up, then back and down. As you do this, the weight is transferred forward onto the front leg so that the right knee bends and the left knee is lowered almost to the beam. Left arm is extended to the side; right arm is in middle back position. Take a large enough step forward so that you can pull the left leg inward and under as you lower the torso into the kneeling position. Chest is lifted, and focus is out.

2. Without stopping, lift yourself back out of the kneeling position, continuing to transfer the weight onto the right leg as you stand in *relevé* position. Meanwhile, bring the left leg forward to a low front position (about 60 degrees) as you toss the right arm forward to front middle. Torso is twisted slightly to the left. The top of the foot brushes along the beam as you lift out of the kneeling position and extend the left leg forward.

   Be sure to move smoothly from the step, down to the kneel, and to the lift out of the kneel position (suggested timing on this movement would be one count down and one count out of the position).

3. Run, run (LR), brush left forward into switch-leg leap, and land on right leg in *plié*, with left leg in *arabesque* position. Left arm is forward with palm up and elbow slightly bent; right arm is extended to straight side position. Be sure to show the *arabesque* position on the landing of the switch-leg leap. Hold the chest and upper back erect.

4. Deepen the *plié* as you take the right arm back to a diagonal back-and-down position. Immediately pivot to the left on the right leg, turning the leg in the socket so that the left leg is now in front. The left hip and shoulder must pull back toward the left as the leg rotates in the socket. The torso twists slightly to the left as the left leg reaches forward. As you do this, *relevé* on the right leg and straighten the knees while pulling the left shoulder back as you pivot, moving the left arm to straight side position. Meanwhile, the right arm presses down along the side of the right leg and up to middle front position with the palm up. Left hip and shoulder must pull back toward the left as the left leg rotates in the socket. The torso twists slightly to the left as the left leg reaches forward.

Problem 2, Solution C

1. Run, run (RL), brush right forward into switch-leg leap. As you land onto the left, continue to transfer the weight forward so as you lower torso, you are in a squat position. In this position, the left knee is bent and the right leg is tucked under you in a kneeling position. Arms are straight side on the leap. The lowering to the squat position must be very controlled. The chest must be extended upward to compensate for the momentous effects from the leap as the torso is lowered. Strongly straighten the base leg and pivot 1/2-turn to the right as the right leg lifts to parallel *passé* position. Right leg extends straight front after the 1/2-turn. Arms remain to the side.

2. Step forward on right and *assemblé* with left. Leave the left arm extended to the side; the right drops to side of leg, then lifts forward to front middle position with palm up on the *assemblé*. There is a slight torso twist to left so that the body is facing out, away from the beam.

3. Step back and to side with right leg. Lift arms up, overhead, and down to right as you take the side step. Transfer weight back onto the left leg as you again face end of beam. Immediately swing right leg 90 degrees to front. *Fouetté* to left to swing the right leg down and front as you face opposite end of beam (leg remains at 90 degrees and arms are held in straight side position as you execute the *fouetté*).

4. Step forward on right. Bring left together to right for jump tuck. Arms optional on jump tuck position.

Creating Timing Variations

Due to limited space as well as a lack of musical accompaniment, there is less concern with distinctive movement style during the composition of beam routines than during similar work on floor. This is not to say that one cannot impose strict interpretation of style in choreographing these routines. However, a less limiting approach, offering a blending of styles that emphasize other concerns, may meet with more success.

For your convenience, five short sample movement phrases of a contemporary, lyrical style are offered here. The counts are added only to serve as a guide for understanding the timing of each phrase. This will help prevent the movement from being performed in a monotonous fashion.

Variation 1

Movement Phrase

1. Stand at end of beam in lunge position with the left leg forward, arms overhead in high fifth position. Straighten arms. Execute an inward circle *port de bra* so that the arms cross in front of the torso as they drop to a low center position. Then lift them up and open to straight side (second position).
2. As the arms lift to second position, twist the torso and hips to the left so that the right hip turns into the left leg and the torso tilts to side right. Note that arms remain in second but appear on a diagonal, the left arm higher than the right, because of the overall tilt position. Focus is right and toward hand.

Count 1 2 3

Hold.

Count 4

3. Straighten torso and bring right arm to high fifth position as you kneel onto the right knee. You are now facing sideways on beam.

Count 5

4. Sweep right arm sideways toward the left. Then circle right arm down and to right to reach for beam as you sit onto the right hip.

Count 6

5. Lean slightly to the right onto the right hand as you extend the left leg above 90 degrees to side. As you do this, change focus to left and extend the left arm to straight side diagonal up position parallel to the line of the left leg.

Count 7 8

6. Bend the left leg to lower the foot to beam; you are now facing the opposite end of beam from which you began. Strongly sweep arms down, then up through first position to high fifth position. Meanwhile, transfer the weight onto the left leg to stand, finishing on a straight left leg with the right leg pointed to the back. As the weight is shifted over the left leg, the right leg extends back so that you pass through a deep lunge position as you stand.

Count 1 2 3 4

7. Circle both arms back, down, then forward to finish in a parallel middle front, upward curve position as the base leg bends and the right leg lifts to *arabesque*.

Count 5 6 7 8

Variation 2

Movement Phrase

1. Stand in lunge position with left leg forward and arms in diagonal up-and-back position. Torso is facing end of beam. Lift the chest and arch the upper back as far as possible while still maintaining the diagonal arm position.

Count 1 2

Recover to an upright position with the arms overhead as you straighten the left leg.

Count 3

Circle both arms forward, down, back, and up to original diagonal back position.

Count 4

2. Deepen the lunge as you continue to circle the arms forward, ending in a middle box position as well as upper torso contraction with the head down.

Count 5 6

3. Strongly transfer the weight over the back leg as you straighten the front leg. Recover from the contraction, lifting the left leg 90 degrees in front. Arms are still in middle box position, and focus is out.

Count 7

Quickly bend the left knee, placing the foot in parallel *passé* position beside the right knee. Circle both arms down and back to diagonal back-and-up position as you *relevé* on the right foot and shift the hips forward. In this position, you are momentarily balanced in an arch, the hips pressed forward and the diagonally back-and-up position of the arms serving as a counterbalance.

Count 8

4. Fall forward onto the left leg in forward lunge. Immediately bring the right hand to the right shoulder to press forward with flexed wrist to straight middle front.

Count 1

Repeat the same action with the left arm.

Count 2

5. Pivot to the right on left foot to face opposite end of beam. As you do this, lift right leg 90 degrees to front and open arms to straight second position with flexed wrists.

Count 3 4

Variation 3

Movement Phrase

1. Stand in parallel first position with hands down at your sides. Face sideways on beam. Step into a parallel side lunge with the right leg. At the same time, with a large, sweeping movement circle the right arm out to the side and overhead. Be focusing to the left and stretching the torso into a side arc position (torso is

arched sideways so that the ribs are expanded to the right and the left side of the body is in a side contraction). Left arm lifts to second position. Right foot is in forced arch position.

Count 1 2

2. Allow right arm to fall forward as right shoulder contracts; left arm is straight and parallel to beam. Continue sweeping the right arm down and back toward the right foot. As you do this, straighten right leg and torso while pivoting on the left foot to face the right foot. As the torso pivots, the left arm moves through the side position and finishes forward middle; the right arm moves through the side position to finish middle back.

Count 3 4

3. Bend the base leg. Quickly lift the right leg 90 degrees to front. At the same time, the right arm swings forward to clasp the left hand and the torso contracts. Focus is out, and both arms are straight.

Count 5

Bend the right leg to parallel *passé* and bend the elbows so that the clasped hands move into chest (elbows lifted).

Count -and

Strongly thrust the right leg back out to front middle position as you forcefully press both arms to middle front position with flexed wrists. This movement should be explosive.

Continue moving so that the arms lift straight overhead as the torso *fouettés* to the left. You are now facing the opposite end of the beam, with the right leg raised into *arabesque* and the arms stretched overhead.

Count 6

4. Fall forward, swinging the right leg forward to a small lunge position.

Count 7

5. Allow the hips to twist to the right as you extend the left leg forward, ending with the leg raised above 90 degrees to second. As you do this, the left arm moves to straight side, and the right arm circles forward and down, ending in a side position. Also end with a torso tilt to the right and the focus right and down.

Count 8

Variation 4

Movement Phrase

1. Stand facing the end of beam in parallel first position with the arms down at your sides. Step forward on the right foot as you lasso the left arm overhead.

Count 1

Press the right arm back and diagonally down to swing forward and up to middle front. Meanwhile, lift the left leg forward above 90 degrees and bend the base leg. Left arm is straight side position, and torso slightly twists to the left, as the right arm reaches forward toward the left foot.

Count 2

Hold.

Count 3

2. Step forward on the left foot; *assemblé* with the right. Arms are straight side.

Count 4 5

3. Immediately perform a *sissonne* forward with a 1/2-turn to the right, changing legs: As you spring into the air and turn toward the right, take the left leg forward and the right leg back into *arabesque*. The landing is on the left leg, the right leg raised to the back. Right arm goes to straight front middle, and left arm goes to side diagonal back position.

Count 6

4. Take a large step back with the right leg onto a straight leg and in *relevé*. Lift the left leg through turned-out *passé*, falling slightly backward as you step down onto the beam just behind the right leg. As you step back, the left arm goes to straight side and the right arm sweeps down, back, and overhead to arrive in high fifth as the leg passes through *passé*. As the left leg steps back onto the beam, the right arm moves forward into first position.

Count 7 8

5. Repeat this backward step with *passé* on the same leg.

Count 1 2

6. Take a step onto the right leg, turning 1/2 to the right to face the opposite end of the beam. Execute a double *pirouette* to the right on the right leg.

Count 3 4

Variation 5

Movement Phrase

1. Stand in parallel first position, facing the end of beam with the arms down at sides. Step forward onto the left foot and perform a high kick with arch release: Right knee lifts as high as possible to the front, then quickly extends to a high kick. At the top of the kick, the upper torso quickly releases back into an arch position while still maintaining the lifted leg to the front. Arms are diagonally back and down. Base leg is straight and in *relevé*. Note that in this movement there is a moment when the torso is straight and the leg is in a very high position, coming just before the arch release.

Count -and 1

2. Allow the right leg to return to the beam as you transfer your weight onto the right leg and recover from the arch release.

Count 2

3. Take a triplet running step with a full turn: Reach forward with the left foot, taking a large step as you face sideways on the beam; allow the torso to pivot to the right so you can continue stepping backward with the right foot; continue pivoting, this time to the right on the right foot as you take the final step forward with the left foot. These all should be fairly large steps. You will complete one full rotation as you travel forward with the three steps.

Count 3-and 4

4. *Assemblé*, brushing the right foot forward. Arms are second position.

Count 5

5. Jump, tuck.

Count 6

6. Brush the right foot forward. Then step on right and extend the left back to pointed position on the beam, right leg slightly bent and arms crossed in front of chest.

Count 7 8

Summary

Improvisation can be an excellent method for stimulating your creativity. Very often we allow ourselves to be limited by the standard steps and poses in our movement vocabularies or by those we see performed by other gymnasts. Acting out situations or experiences such as the sample improvisational problems given in this chapter can help you find new movements and poses that you might not have thought of otherwise.